THE AWFUL
REVOLUTION

THE AWFUL REVOLUTION

The Decline of the Roman Empire
in the West

F. W. WALBANK

*Professor of Ancient History and
Classical Archaeology in the
University of Liverpool*

LIVERPOOL UNIVERSITY PRESS
1969

Published in Great Britain by

LIVERPOOL UNIVERSITY PRESS

Copyright © 1969 by F. W. Walbank

No part of this book may be reproduced
in any form without permission from
the publisher, except for the quotation
of brief passages in criticism

85323 030 7 Cloth
85323 040 4 Paper

First published 1969

Printed and bound in Great Britain by
Hazell Watson and Viney Ltd
Aylesbury, Bucks

TO
JAKE LARSEN

PREFACE

THIS book has had a somewhat curious history. It first appeared as a short essay, written during the War and published in 1946 by the Cobbett Press as Volume III in a series 'Past and Present: Studies in the History of Civilisation'. In 1953 it was reprinted as a paperback in the United States, but both these editions have been out of print for several years. Subsequently I expanded it to deal more fully with the important developments of the fourth and fifth centuries; but this version has hitherto appeared only in a Japanese translation by Dr. Tadasuke Yoshimura, published in Tokyo in 1963.

In response to many enquiries and with the encouragement of the Liverpool University Press, this fuller version now appears in English. The text has again been carefully revised to take account of recent work. In order to avoid confusion with the 1946 volume it seemed better to give a fresh title to what is virtually a new book.

F. W. WALBANK

Liverpool, 1968

CONTENTS

ILLUSTRATIONS

treadmill linked with a system of ropes and pulleys. (Photo: Mansell Collection)

Between pages 90–91

Transport of wine. Bas-relief from Langres showing a pair of mules drawing a large barrel on a four-wheeled cart. Note the primitive harness and absence of a collar. (From M. Rostovtzeff, *Social and Economic History of the Roman Empire*, Oxford, 1957)

Isis Giminiana. This drawing from a fresco from a tomb at Ostia, and now in the Vatican, shows the 'Isis Giminiana', a river craft (*navis codiciaria*) plying between Ostia and Rome, being loaded with grain, which is measured as it is poured into a sack. Farnaces, the ship's captain, stands at the stern. (Institut de Rome, *Annales* 1866, xxxviii and M. Rostovtzeff, *Social and Economic History of the Roman Empire*, Oxford, 1957)

The Arch of Constantine. Erected in Rome in 315 to celebrate the emperor's Christian victory over Maxentius; its carefully worded inscription avoids giving offence to the pagan majority. (From M. Rostovtzeff, *Social and Economic History of the Roman Empire*, Oxford, 1957)

Reliefs from the Arch. These show the emperor addressing the people and distributing money; on the oriental influence revealed in the arrangement of the figures see p. 105.

Bishapur. This shows the victory of the Sassanid king, Sapor I, over the Roman emperor Valerian; the technique parallels that of the reliefs on the Arch of Constantine. (Photo: Professor R. Ghirshman)

Aurei. The three lower coins are *aurei* struck by Maximian (*b*), Galerius (*c*) and Licinius (*d*); the last shows the emperor standing between two conquered barbarians. The large gold medallion (*a*) shows the emperor Constantine in imperial dress (*obverse*) and standing with a globe and consular sceptre (*reverse*). (From M. Rostovtzeff, *Social and Economic History of the Roman Empire*, Oxford, 1957)

ACKNOWLEDGEMENT for permission to reproduce illustrations from the works of M. Rostovtzeff is made to The Clarendon Press, Oxford, and for permission to reproduce other illustrations, to the following: Impressions Rotatives J. Combier à Mâcon; Museo Provinciale Campano, Capua; The Mansell Collection; and Professor R. Ghirshman

INTRODUCTION

ROME first emerges into the light of history as a settlement of traders and farmers inhabiting a group of low hills on the left bank of the River Tiber about fifteen miles from its mouth. Tradition had it that from the foundation of the city in 753 B.C. until 509 B.C. it was governed by kings, the last of them an alien dynasty from Etruria across the Tiber. Of this period little has survived beyond legend; but there is some evidence that Etruscan Rome was a prosperous and beautiful place, more flourishing than at any time during the next century and a half. The hundred and fifty years after the expulsion of the kings were in fact spent in wars with neighbouring peoples and especially in consolidating Roman power in Latium, the district of Italy of which Rome formed, geographically and linguistically, the northern outpost. Her progress received a serious setback in 390 B.C. when marauding Gauls penetrated the city of Rome, sacking and plundering; but she quickly recovered and by 338 B.C. was established as mistress of Latium.

The next seventy years have been described as the most amazing period in Roman history. In a series of successful campaigns the Romans defeated the sturdy highland tribes of central Italy, the Samnites, reduced Etruria to dependence, and obtained access to the Adriatic (338–290 B.C.). By this impressive extension of power the people of an area covering about 500 square miles had made themselves masters of a region a hundred times that size. Shortly afterwards, in 282 B.C., trouble flared up with Tarentum, the prosperous Greek city in the 'instep' of Southern Italy. The Tarentines, long unaccustomed to fighting their own wars, called in the help of the Greek king, Pyrrhus of Epirus, and the Romans found themselves confronted by the greatest general of the generation after Alexander the Great. But Pyrrhus let himself be deflected to Sicily, and upon returning to Italy in 275 B.C. he suffered a decisive defeat, and eventually retired to Epirus, leaving the Romans masters of the whole peninsula.

Thus by 270 B.C. Rome had done what no Greek city-state ever did; by her political acumen, in first separating her enemies and then attaching them to herself, she had welded a vast peninsula into a single unified state. Federal states had existed before, but nothing like this Roman confederacy. Of the various peoples of Italy some, such as the Hernici, Sabines, and other close neighbours of Rome, were incorporated in the Roman state, as citizens. The rest became 'allies', each linked to Rome on separate terms, which served to conceal the harsh reality of Roman domination. To the most favoured the Romans granted Latin citizenship, a status with many but not all of the privileges of the full citizen; other states had special treaties defining their exact relationship with the mistress city; and superimposed on all this were the strategic road system and the carefully placed colonies, which protected Roman interests at any weak point. These were of two types—a limited number of Roman colonies, consisting of full citizens, 300 strong, and rather more Latin colonies, with between 2,000 and 5,000 citizens each, some Latin and some Roman in origin, and designed to function rather as permanent settlements. These new colonies of farmers and soldiers helped to unify and consolidate the peninsula within the bonds of a firm, flexible and loyal alliance. But they did more than that. By diffusing some 50,000 men throughout Italy, they stimulated agriculture and gave the Romans a chance to invest in real estate in all parts of the peninsula. It was probably this period which determined the destiny of the Romans as an agricultural people; and the next seventy years, with their continuation of the same policy of colonization, confirmed it.

This expansion had taken place under the guidance of a narrow council of elder statesmen, the Roman Senate, which formed the element of continuity in a state where the executive officers were amateurs elected annually. The first two and a half centuries of the Republic (509–287 B.C.) saw a protracted but curiously moderated conflict between a 'patrician' minority of rich and aristocratic clans, and the poorer or less privileged 'plebeians'. This conflict was solved in a typical compromise, by which the richer plebeians were absorbed into the ruling group, with equal rights to hold all magistracies and all but a few priesthoods, while the economic demands of the poorer classes were either shelved or diverted towards the plunder of foreign wars.

These were not long in coming. In 264 B.C., having reached the tip of the Italian peninsula, the Romans clashed with the North African Phoenician state of Carthage, which was already established in western Sicily. Carthage was in most ways the antithesis of Rome, a naval power basing its wealth and influence on

trade, never secure of the allegiance of its Moorish subjects, and
so relying on mercenaries to fight its wars. With dogged perse-
verance the Romans took to the sea and with the support of their
confederacy defeated the Carthaginians after a war which lasted
twenty-three years. They emerged in 241 B.C. with a new province,
Sicily, and shortly afterwards annexed Sardinia. In 218 B.C. the
Carthaginians again threw out a challenge. Based on their new
province of Spain and led by a military genius, Hannibal, a
Carthaginian army invaded Italy over the western Alps. For sixteen years Rome fought a struggle for existence on Italian soil.
But the Senate kept its head in crisis after crisis, the confederacy
held, Spain was cut off from Hannibal by the landing of a Roman
expeditionary force, upward of forty legions—reaching as many
as twenty-five in a single year—were eventually enrolled from
among the peasant stock of Italy, and finally under a great general,
Scipio Africanus, the Romans themselves invaded North Africa,
forced the return of Hannibal and inflicted a crushing defeat
(202 B.C.) from which Carthage never recovered.

Now, on the threshold of the second century B.C., the Romans
turned east. In a series of wars which they did not deliberately
seek, but which from a mixture of motives they were generally
ready to undertake, the Senate crushed the separate Hellenistic
monarchies, which had arisen out of the breakup of Alexander
the Great's unwieldy empire. Philip V of Macedon (197 B.C.),
Antiochus of Syria (189 B.C.), Philip's son Perseus (168 B.C.), fell
in turn before the onslaught of legions schooled in the struggle
with Hannibal. Egypt, now weakly ruled and no longer a great
power, was brought into the sphere of Roman influence. The great
commercial city of Rhodes, at first the favourite of Rome, in-
curred her ill-will and was shorn of her possessions. The Achaeans,
formerly the most loyal of Roman allies, revolted and were put
down (146 B.C.). Macedon became a province, and Achaea
virtually one. The kingdom of Pergamum in north-west Asia
Minor was bequeathed to Rome by her last king (133 B.C.). Meanwhile Carthage had been wiped out in a bloody and unprovoked
war of aggression (146 B.C.); and farther west, in Spain, the last
resistance of the tribes was broken at Numantia, in 133 B.C., by the
younger Scipio, the conqueror of Carthage.

Thus by 133 B.C. Rome was predominant in eastern and western
Mediterranean alike. No longer was there any power capable of

resisting her. The Greek historian Polybius, himself an Achaean and for many years a political prisoner at Rome, was converted to admiration for this vast empire, acquired in the main in just over fifty years (220–167 B.C.), as if the goddess Fortune herself were planning the fate of the civilized world along the lines traced by the Roman legions; and his history survives (though fragmentarily) as a permanent record of the impression made by the advancing Romans upon the peoples they overcame.

But for all this there was a price to pay. The sixteen years of Hannibal had been disastrous for Italian agriculture. Farms were ravaged, farmers sent off marching in the legions year after year. Then came the new wars in the east. With the peasantry ruined or disheartened the way was open to the wealthy, who had speculated in the wars and, as the most influential Roman writers advocated, sought to buy respectability in the form of land. The second century B.C. saw the growth of large *latifundia*, sheep ranches and plantations, all over Southern Italy, Etruria, Latium, and parts of Campania, worked by cheap slaves provided by the wars. The dispossessed peasantry drifted into the towns to swell the urban proletariat and live uprooted lives on the margin of poverty. At the other end of the scale the vast fortunes which poured into Italy from the East (after 167 B.C. Italy was freed for ever from the paying of tribute) led to the corruption of the ruling caste. The Senate remained narrow in composition. Between 264 and 134 B.C., out of 262 elected consuls only 16 sprang from families new to the office. There was little new blood here, and thus, when corruption crept in, its effects were catastrophic. Several discreditable incidents in the isolated and difficult province of Spain revealed a decay in the standards of morality among the rulers of Rome. Contact with the higher culture of Greece was leading to a radical change in their ways of thought but, as Polybius noted from his own observation, and as generations of Roman moralists and satirists were never tired of pointing out, it had also brought greater luxury and greater laxity of behaviour. The allies of the Italian confederacy began to complain of the growing stinginess and oppression of the leading state; and in one way or another the inadequacy of the Roman aristocracy for the task of governing an empire was becoming increasingly apparent.

The last century of the Roman Republic, from 133 to 31 B.C., was essentially an age of crisis; and to this crisis many factors contributed. The curtain went up on a noteworthy attempt by the two brothers Gracchus, Tiberius in 133 B.C. and Gaius in 123 B.C., to solve the problem of big estates and dispossessed peasantry by a radical distribution of nominally public land. The oligarchs reacted quickly. Tiberius was murdered, Gaius driven to suicide and the senatorial class resumed its sway. But out of the Gracchan agitation a new class arose to rival the Senate in its monopoly of power. The bequest of Pergamum to the Roman Republic in the year of Tiberius Gracchus's tribunate had provided a new problem of organization; and it was partly a reluctance to create new machinery which led to the adoption of the system of farming out the collection of the taxes to financial companies. The social group which undertook this lucrative business was that of the *Equites* or Knights; and their corporations gained wealth and power from these Asiatic contracts. To this C. Gracchus added political influence, when he placed in their hands the control of the law-courts in which senatorial governors had frequently to meet charges of peculation and extortion. Henceforth the *Equites* have their own role to play in Roman politics; and there is reason to see their malign influence behind the colonial war upon which the Romans embarked towards the end of the century against the Numidian tribes of North Africa under their king Jugurtha (112–106 B.C.). This war revealed unparalleled depths of senatorial corruption and incompetence. Jugurtha is said to have cynically pronounced all Rome 'for sale'; a 'new man', Marius, rode on popular support into the consulship, defeated the Numidians and carried out a series of army reforms, the result of which was to fill the legions from the rural proletariat and to elevate the position of the military commander by making him the personal object of his men's oath of allegiance—an ominous development. Meanwhile the greed and incompetence of the ruling caste allowed the friction between Rome and the Italian confederation to develop to the point of civil war. The Italian revolt took two years to suppress (90–88 B.C.) and brought a new figure into prominence, Sulla, the former lieutenant and bitter foe of Marius. For several years Rome was torn with civil war between their two factions; and in 83 B.C. Sulla returned from an eastern command to make himself sole master of Rome, with the object of restoring the Senate to its ancient role.

We need not trace in detail the further deterioration of senatorial government, the failure of Sulla's attempt to restore the Senate's power and the speedy demolition of his structure by the young Pompey, a successful and precocious general of Sulla's own school, acting together with Crassus, a Senator who represented the business interests of the Knights. These two men had attained an uneasy coalition after their suppression of a slave revolt led by a Thracian gladiator named Spartacus (73–71 B.C.), and their consulship in 70 B.C. was marked by the revelation of senatorial vice and corruption which emerged from the famous trial of Verres, the governor of Sicily, for extortion—a trial which made the name of the rising barrister M. Tullius Cicero. It was Cicero who as consul, seven years later, showed unexpected firmness combined with a dangerous disregard for republican precedent in suppressing Catiline's anarchistic attempt to overthrow the State, and sending the chief conspirators to execution in the dank prison of the Tullianum.

Meanwhile these years saw the rise of a politician tougher and more astute than any of his fellows—C. Julius Caesar. Elected consul in 59 B.C., thanks to a politic alliance with Pompey and Crassus, he obtained a proconsular command in Gaul, and during the next ten years built up a force unswervingly loyal to himself and trained under his brilliant generalship in a hard school of fighting. In 49 B.C., provoked and threatened with prosecution and ruin by a Senate which had learnt nothing and forgotten nothing, he crossed the River Rubicon, the boundary separating his province from Italy, and in a series of brilliant campaigns in Italy, Spain, Greece, Asia Minor and Africa, defeated the forces of the Senate led by his rival and late ally Pompey, and smashed his way to supreme power.

Caesar saw (what was obvious in retrospect) that the survival of Rome and her empire depended at this time on establishing some form of autocracy. But he lacked tact in dealing with those who did not possess this particular form of enlightenment, and on 15 March, 44 B.C., he was murdered by a small band of conspirators, inspired by and largely consisting of Senators. His death was the signal for yet another thirteen years of political manoeuvring and civil war. Caesar's heir and adopted son Octavianus at first came forward as the Senate's man, and won the glowing, if sometimes ambiguous praise of Cicero, who, after a series of political set-backs had emerged to sing the swan-song of the Republic. But very soon Octavian came to terms with the political adventurer, Mark Antony, and their compact was sealed with a bloody proscription, in which Cicero's head was among the first to roll.

The compact between Octavian and Antony did not last; and it was the younger man who outplayed his rival. Octavian was a worthy successor to Julius. Equally ruthless and free from sentiment, he possessed that added insight into Roman susceptibilities which enabled him to conceal his intentions. After Antony by his intrigues with the Egyptian queen, Cleopatra, had given Octavian a chance to brand him before the people as guilty of un-Roman activities and to pursue him in a propaganda campaign in which neither side recognized any limits, Italy was lost to the old Caesarian; and it was finally no hard task to eliminate both Antony and Cleopatra at the much lauded but hardly glorious naval battle of Actium in 31 B.C. Octavian now stood alone; and with the backing of the Caesarian party, which he and his adopted father had sedulously assembled from among the middle classes of Italy, he proceeded to establish a new state. By now the Senate, or what remained of it, was no longer an obstacle; and Octavian, henceforth to be known by the honorific title of Augustus, made great show of taking it into political partnership.

The year 31 B.C. marked the effective setting up of the Empire, the government of the Roman world by its leading citizen (*princeps*) and general (*imperator*). Augustus's first concern was peace and efficiency. The provinces, now enriched with new territories in Asia Minor and Egypt, were divided out between himself and the Senate. Frontiers were consolidated. An efficient instrument of government was devised. Gone were the days of proconsular corruption, when a governor had to make three fortunes during his year's administration, one to pay his debts, another on which to retire, and a third to bribe the jurors in the inevitable trial for extortion. The Roman world at last settled down to peace and prosperity; and it was a prosperity which lasted almost unbroken for over two centuries. Yet from its outset the Augustan principate contained elements of weakness, however cleverly they might be disguised. For all the care which Augustus took to base his position upon republican precedents and on the accumulation of already existing offices and powers exercised in conjunction with that indefinable 'authority', which counted for so much to a people steeped in tradition, there were clear-minded men here and there who recognized the truth—that Augustus's ultimate sanctions lay in his control of the legions. Moreover, so long as the problem of the succession was left open, there was no guarantee of continued peace; yet to establish a dynasty openly was to risk removing the mask of freedom, and so perhaps go the way of Julius.

Fortunately Augustus lived to old age, and gave men a chance to forget the Republic. As they grew used to the disguised monarchy, the disguise became less necessary, and the Roman people ceased to demand even the semblance of freedom. Awake to the dangers of an interregnum, Augustus schemed cautiously but incessantly to establish a dynasty; and his first four successors, Tiberius, Gaius, Claudius and Nero, were all connected with his family. Their characters revealed some of the weaknesses of autocracy. Gaius and Nero at least were victims of the dazzle of power, exercised without restraint; and both met violent ends. On Nero's death in A.D. 68 'a secret of empire was revealed', namely, that emperors might be created outside Rome. The armies of Spain, Germany and Syria each proclaimed its own general emperor, and only after a year of bloody war and chaos, in which four men successively held the purple, was the new Flavian dynasty established. Under Vespasian and his two sons, Titus and Domitian, the autocracy became yet more open; and the latter sought to emulate Gaius, established a reign of terror and was ultimately assassinated (A.D. 96). The selection of a new emperor now reverted to the Senate. Nerva, Trajan and Hadrian brought the Empire a new era of peace and prosperity, which continued under the second century emperors, Antoninus Pius and Marcus Aurelius.

Such, in brief, is the story of how Rome grew from Tiber village to Mediterranean Empire. This empire, like so many others, failed to endure; but on its broken fragments, reshaped and revitalized to suit their own more primitive institutions, the Germanic peoples who overran it in time built up the foundations of a world whose linguistic frontiers in many places still betray the old limits of the *orbis Romanus*, a world in which the legal, ethical and cultural traditions are still in essence the traditions of Greece and Rome.

The Roman Empire fell; and the fall of empires is a romantic and a tragic theme. It was a romantic urge which, on 15 October 1764, inspired Edward Gibbon, as he sat musing amidst the ruins of the Capitol, listening to the bare-footed friars of St. Francis singing their Vespers in the temple of Jupiter,[1] to dedicate his labours to the description of the *Decline and Fall of the Roman Empire* and so to the creation of one of the classics of the English tongue. But as he was at pains to show, the fall of Rome has also a moral to labour and a lesson to teach. 'Past events' wrote Polybius (xii, 25e, 6) 'make us pay particular attention to the future, if we really make thorough enquiry in each case into the past'. It is in the spirit of this pronouncement that the following pages have been written.

1. So he believed. But S. Maria d'Aracoeli, where Gibbon listened to the friars, is on the site of the Temple of Juno Moneta. 'The shrine of Jupiter was on the other side of the Campidoglio, on the slightly lower eminence of the bicorned Capitoline' (L. White, *The Transformation of the Roman World: Gibbon's Problem after Two Centuries* (Berkeley – Los Angeles, 1966), 291.

1

THE NATURE OF THE PROBLEM

SINCE man first learnt to record his own history in a durable
form, he has turned to the records of the past for light upon
the problems of the present; and to certain periods and events
he has referred again and again because they seemed particularly
alive and relevant to his own situation. One such period is that
which saw the downfall of the Roman Empire in Western Europe;
and from the time of the early Christian Fathers up to the present
day the why and wherefore of its decline has been a focal point
of historical speculation. The answers to this problem themselves
form a commentary upon the ages that proposed them. But they
have one thing in common. They show that to the men of
Western Europe the problem of why Rome fell has always been
a *topical* question.

From the beginning of our era onwards the people of the
Empire were obsessed with a vague feeling of deterioration. The
elder Seneca (*c.* 55 B.C. – *c.* A.D. 40), in a historical work now
lost, asserted that under the Emperors Rome had reached its old
age and could look forward to nothing but death;[1] and his
pessimism merely echoed the repeated laments of late Republican
poets and writers that Rome was no longer what she used to be.
Horace, for example, complained that 'our parents' generation,
worse than that of our grandfathers, has brought us forth, more
worthless than they, and soon to produce a brood yet more
vicious'.[2] But by the early third century the government itself
was confessing to the decay of the Empire. An official proclama-
tion, written for the boy-emperor Severus Alexander in A.D. 222
(probably by his mother and grandmother and the jurist Ulpian),
speaks of the Emperor's intention to arrest the decline by a policy
of restriction, at the same time lamenting his inability to gratify
his natural generosity by a remission of taxes; and nearly thirty
years later we read of the expression of similar hopes in connection
with the emperor Decius (A.D. 249 – 51).

With the rise of the Christian Church, however, the decline

1. Lactantius, *Div. Inst.* vii, 15.   2. *Odes*, iii, 6, 46–8.

of Rome began to become a central issue in philosophy and polemic. In such apocalyptic prophecies as *The Book of Revelation* the Roman Empire had been held up to scorn and pilloried by the persecuted Church, and its end foretold as the precursor of the coming millenium. St. Augustine (A.D. 354–430), drawing his ammunition from pre-Christian historians, attacked Rome for her moral decadence; since the destruction of Carthage, her last serious rival, in 146 B.C., her ancient virtues had declined, and the State had been reft asunder by civil discord. Eternal Rome— *Roma aeterna*—was a literary fiction, and Christians must turn their eyes to the City of God. St. Jerome (*c.* A.D. 346–420) was of the same opinion. 'The Roman Empire', he writes, 'must be destroyed because its rulers deem it eternal. On the forehead of eternal Rome is written the name of blasphemy.' Yet this attitude was not without its ambiguities and equivocations. For when the pagans in their turn accused the Church of bringing about the downfall of the Empire by its hostility and disruptive practices, the Church retaliated with a new doctrine. To Orosius (*fl.* A.D. 410), the friend of both Augustine and Jerome, the Empire represented the last of four world-kingdoms—its predecessors being Babylon, Carthage and Macedon—and was designed to be God's instrument for the protection of the Christian world against chaos. Was it not under Augustus that Christ himself had become incarnate—'and a Roman citizen'?[1] Accordingly it became clear that Christians must accept and support the Empire, for on it depended the fate of the universe: as the saying went:

'Quando cadet Roma, cadet et mundus'
(When Rome falls, the universe will fall with it).

A curious feature of this controversy was its treatment of the fall of Rome as an event lying in the future. Not once did any of these pagan or Christian publicists rise up to announce in tones of triumph or regret that Rome had already fallen. When the Eternal City was sacked by Alaric and his Visigoths in A.D. 410, the event was received with incredulous stupefaction—and then rejected. 'If Rome perishes', wrote Jerome himself, 'what is safe?' Orosius was quick to observe that Alaric had only remained three days in Rome—whereas in 390 B.C. Brennus and the Gauls had occupied it for six months! A century later there was less confidence.

1. Orosius, *Hist.* vi, 22,8.

Salvian (*c.* A.D. 400—after A.D. 470), presbyter at Marseilles, writing when wide tracts of the Western Empire were already in the hands of the barbarians, chastises the Romans as being more to blame than their foes precisely because they are Christians and should know better. The barbarians are chaste, while the cities of Rome are sinks of iniquity. In short, what were the barbarian invasions but God's judgement upon an Empire 'already dead or certainly breathing its last'?[1]

Nevertheless, the belief in Rome was never wholly lost. Long after the western Empire had dissolved, men still gave their allegiance to its shadow, conjured up by the fiction of the *translatio ad Francos*—the transference of the Empire to Charlemagne (whom the Pope crowned Emperor on Christmas Day, A.D. 800) and from the tenth century onwards to Otto and the Germans. In the Holy Roman Empire established in Aachen or Goslar people were persuaded to see the lineal descendant of the Rome of Augustus, still fulfilling its role as the 'fourth world kingdom' which should precede the coming of anti-Christ and ultimately the Millenium; and in the Mediterranean lands the gradualness of the change from Latin to the Romance languages helped to obscure the real character of the break. It was not until the Renaissance, when Europe awoke to the treasures of the great ages of Greek and Roman antiquity, that Italian humanists grew conscious of their own break with the middle ages and, consequently, of the break between the middle ages and the ancient world. In A.D. 1453 Biondo divorced himself completely from the idea of the fourth world kingdom, and in his history, entitled significantly *From the Decline of the Roman Empire*, he took Alaric's sack of Rome as marking a historical epoch. Now for the first time the problem of the decline of Rome became a *historical* problem, an attempt to explain an event which already lay in the past.

Again the answers given were topical, reflecting the problems of those who propounded them, and designed to illuminate what was dark in contemporary life. To Petrarch (A.D. 1304–74) the root of all evil lay in Julius Caesar, who destroyed popular liberties; for Petrarch saw his great heroes in Caesar's opponents, Brutus and Pompey, and sought to resuscitate a *respublica Romana* in his own times. Over a century later, in *The Prince*, the Florentine Machiavelli (A.D. 1469–1527) urged the pressing need to

1. Salvian, *de gubern. Dei*, iv, 30.

recreate an Italian State to save Italy. Conscious of the threat from beyond the Alps in his own day, he laid emphasis on the contribution of the barbarian invasions to the downfall of the classical world, which, like Biondo, he dated from Alaric's sack of Rome. Throughout his work there is a sharp sense of the decadence of both his own society and that of ancient Rome; and with his belief in the recurrence of historical events he hopes to point a moral. Machiavelli was the first historian since Polybius in the second century B.C. to pay serious attention to the internal process of decay within society. A little later Paolo Paruta, a Venetian aristocrat, who published his *Discorsi* in A.D. 1599, attributed Roman decay to the tension existing between the Roman Senate and the Roman people.

In the seventeenth century the discussion rid itself of the last traces of the mediaeval concepts of the *translatio ad Francos* and the 'fourth world monarchy'. The fall of Constantinople in 1453 provided a new epoch to set against its foundation by Constantine, and gradually there grew up the concept of ancient, mediaeval, and modern history. However, this new grouping left the heart of the problem untouched; and to Voltaire (A.D. 1694–1778) and Gibbon (A.D. 1737–94) it presented itself in the new context of the age of enlightenment. 'Two flails at last brought down this vast Colossus:' wrote Voltaire, 'the barbarians and religious disputes.' And Gibbon too saw in the long-protracted story of the Decline and Fall 'the triumph of barbarism and religion'. Thus since Augustine's day the wheel had turned full circle: now once more Christianity stood charged in the dock. Gibbon's answer reveals the special circumstances of the eighteenth century, when it seemed to the hasty judgement of the rationalists that Christianity was in decline and must shortly yield to a new world outlook. Naturally they looked back from the end to the beginnings of the Christian cycle and saw in the present decadence of Christianity a contrast to the vigour it had then displayed; and so they felt themselves to be somehow the avengers of the world of reason they believed Christianity to have destroyed.

These examples may serve to illustrate the peculiarly topical shape which the problem of the decline of Rome invariably assumed.

From it each age in turn has tried to formulate its own conception of progress and decadence. What, men have asked repeatedly, is the criterion by which we determine the point at which a society begins to decay? What is the yard-stick by which we are to measure progress? And what are the symptoms and causes of decadence? The variety of answers given to these questions is calculated to depress the enquiring reader. When so many representative thinkers can find so many and such various explanations, according to the age in which they live, is there any hope, he will ask, of an answer that can claim more than purely relative validity?

The problem of progress and decadence (if we may so term it) has indeed evoked a variety of solutions. At some periods, as we have seen—particularly during the Renaissance—the question is broached in terms of political issues; society goes forward or back according to how it settles questions of popular liberty, the power of the State, the existence of tensions within its own structure. At other times the moral note is struck: decay appears as a decline in ethical standards, whether through the removal of salutary threats from without or through the incursion of luxury. Both these approaches are essentially 'naturalistic' in that they attempt to deduce the forms of progress and decadence from man's own acts, moral or political; and they stand in contrast to what has, on the whole, been the more usual attitude to the problem— the religious or mystical approach.

By some the rise and fall of empires have been interpreted (as among the early Christians) in prophetic terms, so as to conform with an apocalyptic picture of 'four world kingdoms' or 'six world ages'. Another view treats history as a succession of civilizations, each reproducing the growth and decline of a living organism, in accordance with a kind of biological law. Or again civilizations are regarded as developing in cycles, one following straight after and repeating another, so that history is virtually a revolving wheel. Propounded originally by Plato (c. 427–347 B.C.), this cyclical theory found favour with Polybius (c. 200–117 B.C.), the Greek historian of Rome's rise to power, who thought it explained certain signs of decadence which his keen eye had detected at the height of Roman success. Taken over from Polybius by Machiavelli, this cyclical theory was adapted by G. B. Vico in the eighteenth century, and has its disciples in our own day.

Similarly, the biological conception has become part of the common currency of historical writing. 'The vast fabric,' a modern scholar and statesman has written of the Roman Empire,[1] 'succumbed in time, as all human institutions do, to the law of decay'. Such a formulation employs metaphor to evade the real problem.

These various answers seem largely to depend on where one starts. And perhaps the most satisfactory starting-point is the body which itself progresses and decays. For progress and decay are functions, not of isolated individuals, but of men and women knit together in society. It is society which goes forward or backward; and civilization is essentially a quality of social man, as Aristotle saw when he defined the state as originating in the bare needs of life and continuing in existence for the sake of the good life.[2] The distinction is important, for an age of social decline, such as the third century of our era, may well—indeed often, by reason of the very challenge which it offers, does—produce an unusually large number of outstanding individuals. Evidently, therefore, when we say a society is in decay, we refer to something having gone wrong within its structure, or in the relationship between the various groups which compose it. The problem of decadence, like the problem of progress, is at the root a problem of man in society.

Now it is precisely this fact which gives ground for hoping that to-day it may be possible to say something new about the problem of the decline of the Roman Empire. For it is in our knowledge of the social man of antiquity that there has been the greatest revolution in the classical studies of the last sixty years.

In the past, ancient history was inevitably subjected to a double distortion. Our knowledge of the past could come in the main only from the writers of the past. In the last resort historians were dependent on their literary sources, and had to accept, roughly speaking, the world these drew. In addition there was the bias which the historian himself invariably imports into what he writes, rendered the more dangerous because he could let his fancy play, with no external control beyond those literary sources.

1. H. H. Asquith in *The Legacy of Rome*, ed. Cyril Bailey, Oxford, 1923, p. 1.
2. *Politics*, i, 2, 8. 1252 b.

To-day the picture is quite different. For over fifty years classical scholars of many nationalities have been busy digging, classifying and interpreting material which was never meant for the historian's eye, and is for that reason invaluable evidence about the age which produced it. The buried towns of Pompeii and Herculaneum, with their houses, shops, and equipment, had already attracted the sporadic attention of excavators in the eighteenth century. More recently they have been systematically investigated and their lessons amplified and modified by similar work at Ostia at the Tiber mouth, and by excavations on ancient sites in every part of the Empire. The information now available is enormous. Inscriptions set up to embody some government decree in Athens or Ephesus, or to record some financial transaction on Delos, or the manumission of a slave at Delphi; the dedication of countless soldiers to their favourite deity, Mithras or perhaps some purely local goddess, like Coventina at Carrawburgh in Northumberland; papyrus fragments of household accounts and the libraries of great houses, salvaged from the sand of Oxyrhyncus and the mummy-cases of Roman Egypt—all these separate fragments of evidence are being constantly assembled, catalogued and interpreted in the light of what was already known. The shelves of libraries in every country are filled with the vast *corpora* of inscriptions and papyri, the detailed accounts of individual excavations and countless monographs in which the results are assessed. All this has opened up new vistas for the historian of social and economic life.

Now for the first time it is possible to turn a microscope on the ancient world. From the consideration of thousands of separate instances, general trends have been deduced, statistical calculations have been made. We can now see beyond the individual to the life of society as a whole; and with that change in perspective we are able to determine directions where the literary sources showed us none. This does not, of course, mean that the classical authors may now be neglected. On the contrary they have become doubly valuable, for the light they throw on (and receive from) the new evidence. For consecutive history we still depend on the literary sources with their personal details; but the new discoveries give them a new dimension, particularly in all that concerns social or 'statistical' man. Much of the bias of our sources had thereby been overcome; and though the presuppositions of the historian himself survive as an indissoluble residuum, the scientific, indisputable' character of the new evidence frequently controls the answer, like the materials of a laboratory experiment. Thus for the first time in history it has become possible to analyse the course of decay in the Roman world with some degree of objectivity.

NOTES FOR FURTHER READING

Perhaps the best introduction to the problem is Gibbon's *Decline and Fall of the Roman Empire*, ed. J. B. Bury, chapters 1–3, with the appendix included after chapter 38. For recent surveys of some of the many proposed solutions see M. Cary, *A History of Rome down to the Time of Constantine*, London, 1935, pp. 771–9 (a useful manual of Roman history); an article by N. H. Baynes in *Journal of Roman Studies*, 1943, pp. 29–35; M. Rostovtzeff, *Social and Economic History of the Roman Empire*, second ed. revised by P. M. Fraser, Oxford, 1957, vol. I, pp. 502–41; and A. Piganiol, *L'empire chrétien* (325–95), Vol. IV, 2 of Glotz's *Histoire romaine*, Paris, 1957, pp. 411–22. Those interested in a detailed discussion from an idealistic point of view of the problem of decline and fall may consult A. J. Toynbee, *A Study in History*, Oxford, 1934–54, 10 volumes, a vast work on an 18th-century scale (volume four deals specifically with the problem of decline), or Oswald Spengler, *The Decline of the West*, tr. Atkinson, London 1926–8, a work that is often 'mystical' and perverse, frequently unreliable as to facts, but always thought-provoking. The materialistic point of view is put forward in J. M. Robertson's little-known but acute and significant study, *The Evolution of States*, London, 1912. Two recent surveys: D. Kagan, *Decline and Fall of the Roman Empire*, Boston, 1962, and M. Chambers, *The Fall of Rome; can it be explained?* New York, 1963, contain extracts from a number of writers on this topic and useful bibliography. The most convenient treatment of the problem of how the idea of Rome, its decline and its survival, have appeared to various ages and generations is in a German book, W. Rehm, *Der Untergang Roms im abendländischen Denken: ein Beitrag zur Geschichtsschreibung und zum Dekadenzproblem*, Vol. xviii of the series 'Das Erbe der Alten', Leipzig, 1930.

2

THE INDIAN SUMMER OF
THE ANTONINES

IT was the belief of Edward Gibbon, who made the age of the
Antonines the starting-point of his *Decline and Fall of the Roman
Empire*, that the peoples of Europe were never happier than
under the 'five good Emperors'—Nerva (A.D. 96–98), Trajan (A.D.
98–117), Hadrian (A.D. 117–38), Antoninus Pius (A.D. 138–61) and
Marcus Aurelius (A.D. 161–80). In support of this view one can
appeal to contemporary testimony. Tertullian (*c.* A.D. 160 – *c.*
A.D. 225), no friend to pagan Rome, writes:

The world is every day better known, better cultivated and more civilized
than before. Everywhere roads are traced, every district is known, every
country opened to commerce. Smiling fields have invaded the forests; flocks
and herds have routed the wild beasts; the very sands are sown; the rocks are
broken up; the marshes drained. There are now as many cities as there were
formerly cottages. Reefs and shoals have lost their terrors. Wherever there
is a trace of life there are houses, human habitations, and well-ordered
governments.[1]

The rhetorical colouring of this passage and of such a panegyric
as the famous speech 'On Rome' by Aelius Aristides (A.D. 117–89)
must not be overlooked. Nevertheless, the Empire of A.D. 150 can
at first sight make a strong claim to be regarded as the high-water
mark of ancient civilization. A vast area around the Mediterranean,
which had long been linked together economically, had now been
wrought into a single political unit. This work had begun when
Alexander the Great led his Graeco-Macedonian army across the
Hellespont to overthrow the Persian Empire, and dying ten years
later (323 B.C.), left behind him a world of national states—Macedon, Egypt, Syria; it was completed in the second and first centuries
B.C., when these successor states fell one after the other before the
advancing legions of the Roman Republic. What the Republic
won, the Caesars consolidated; Gaul, Spain, Britain and Africa
were added to the Greek states; and by the time of Hadrian the

1. Tertullian, *de anima*, 30.

Empire embraced an area of unparalleled extent within a single economic and political system.

To the north it found a natural frontier on the Rhine and the Danube, linked together by a fortified line of camps, the *limes*, stretching from a little below Cologne to a point just west of Regensburg. In Britain the frontier was defined by a wall from Bowness-on-Solway to Wallsend-on-Tyne, except for a short time in the second century A.D., when it was advanced to the Forth-Clyde line. Further east it swept north of the Danube to include Dacia (modern Roumania), leaving however a narrow funnel of unconquered territory between the Danube and the Theiss, north-west of Singidunum (Belgrade). On the west the authority of Rome reached the Atlantic, on the east the Euphrates and the desert; for Trajan's annexations in Armenia and Mesopotamia were at once abandoned by his successor, Hadrian. To the south Egypt, Cyrenaica, Africa, Numidia and Mauretania formed a continuous string of provinces from the Red Sea to the Atlantic, with the Sahara as their southern limit.

This huge area, within its well-devised frontiers, was a single economic unit, capable—with a few exceptions—of satisfying its own needs. From the setting-up of the Principate by Augustus (the former Octavian) after Mark Antony's defeat at Actium in 31 B.C., the Empire enjoyed all the blessings of the *pax Romana* for close on a quarter of a millenium. Freed from the fears and burdens of foreign war, its people could devote themselves to peaceful pursuits, commerce, industry, agriculture. Piracy was almost unknown: and on land good roads facilitated travel. Culturally and politically, the Empire was a unity; in the west Latin, which made great strides everywhere, and in the east the Greek *koine*, the language of the New Testament, afforded the various peoples a common instrument of communication. And the coining of the word *humanitas*—'human decency'—by Cicero (106–43 B.C.) coincided with a spread in humanitarian sentiment, linked ultimately with the Stoic belief in the common brotherhood of all men, whatever their race or status. Finally, in the legal concept of the *civis Romanus*, the 'citizen of no mean city' who, though perhaps a Gaul or a Syrian by birth, and still in enjoyment of his local citizenship, was also a Roman in the eyes of the law, the Empire produced a class of subjects whose political status transcended frontier and race. The *cives Romani* were, in theory (and to a large extent, in fact), a leaven spreading culture and Romanization throughout the vast territories governed by the Emperor; and not least important, the institution of Roman citizenship itself, with its carefully distinguished grades and recognized channels by which the provincials might rise from one to another, was a device making for ultimate equality, and provided the peoples of the Empire with an incentive to both imperial and municipal patriotism.

The quickening of economic and cultural life which followed the establishment of the *pax Romana* was indeed everywhere associated with an increase in the number of cities and the prosperity of the city bourgeoisie.

This social stratum was mainly composed of the soldiery and their descendants, or derived from other sections of the citizen-farmer class—Roman, Greek or sometimes non-Greek in origin; a considerable percentage consisted of freedmen, mostly of Greek nationality, who had a flair for business and had become wealthy . . .; and the knights also, being recruited largely from the municipal aristocracy, which in its turn drew on the bourgeoisie, are to be counted in this class. It was, then, the active business section of the community, deeply interested in industry and trade, which now grew in importance.[1]

This city bourgeoisie was the instrument of the spread of city life over the new areas of Britain, north and central Gaul, and Spain, where hitherto life had been mainly organized on a tribal or cantonal basis.

In the third century B.C. after Alexander, the Greek bourgeoisie had peopled the Near and Middle East with Greek cities, spreading Hellenic culture and Hellenic values as far as the Indus and the Jaxartes. The cities of the Hellenistic world were large even by modern standards. In A.D. 6/7 Apamea in Syria had a population of 117,000 full citizens, so that its total population may well have reached 500,000. The same figure probably applied to Antioch and Alexandria, and towns of 100,000 and more were common. This achievement the Italian bourgeoisie now duplicated in the west, directed and assisted by the Emperors, who thus carried on the civilizing work of the Hellenistic kings. Their help and direction

1. F. Oertel in *Cambridge Ancient History*, Vol. X (1934), p. 388.

were forthcoming in the east as well as the west; in the cities of the eastern half of the Empire the setting up of the Principate is marked by the appearance of new buildings, the revival of festivals, and the resuscitation of local coinages. But even more remarkable—and especially so under the Flavian emperors (A.D. 69–96), who in some degree reacted against the philhellenism of their predecessors—was the rapid civilizing of the newer lands of the west. Romanization soon made its mark in the creation of such cities as Timgad (Thaumugadi) in N. Africa, Caerwent, Cirencester, London and Colchester in Britain, Autun and Vaison in Gaul, and Trier and Heddernheim (near Frankfurt-am-Main) in Roman Germany. These cities, varying from 20 to 500 acres in size, possessed each its forum and public buildings, well-planned and commodious, with shops and residential blocks, and usually public baths and theatres. They brought new life to countries like Gaul and Britain, which had hitherto known nothing better than the squalid settlements of the La Tène culture.[1]

In all this there was an element of improvisation. In both the east and west we find provincial councils established as centres for the worship of the emperors and the spread of Romanization; but in the east particularly, where councils had already existed before the Roman conquest, these were now adapted to Roman purposes. There was, indeed, no uniformity. But one significant trend is worth observing. Within the western provinces, following the pattern of Rome and the towns of Italy, the cities were governed by annual magistrates and an all-powerful senate, the members of which were appointed for life; the primary assembly was of negligible importance and the government was oligarchic. But now, under the Empire, in the east too, continuing a process already perceptible in Hellenistic times, the old democratic municipal forms gradually made way for government on the western pattern, a transformation which produced a twofold result: it established power firmly in the hands of the propertied classes, and at the same time prepared the way for later bureaucratic interference.

The municipal and provincial upper class, which was thus strengthened, had risen to power with the decline of the narrow Roman Senate and the aristocratic senatorial class of Roman land-

1. The pre-Roman Iron Age culture in Europe from about 500 B.C. onwards is usually called after the site in Switzerland where it has been most extensively studied.

owners, who were defeated in the civil wars by a coalition between the professional army and the bourgeoisie of Italy, and subsequently all but exterminated under the terror of the Julio-Claudian dynasty from Tiberius to Nero (A.D. 14–68). During the first two centuries of our era the Italian and provincial upper classes were acting in direct alliance with the Emperors in Romanizing and developing the western provinces. But it is noteworthy that in spite of such imperial encouragement this urbanization never reached the intensity of the former Hellenistic wave, and economically the west remained far behind the provinces of Asia Minor and Syria. This factor was ultimately to prove of vital importance, for it meant that the East was to remain more united, more vigorous, and richer than the west, as well as physically more difficult for any invading army to occupy.[1]

One notable feature of the rise of the bourgeoisie under the early Empire was the role played by the State. Whether it was, as one historian suggests,[2] that having inherited a state apparatus which was unequal to the formidable task of organizing an empire, Augustus chose the path of least resistance, or whether, after the crisis of the previous century, he genuinely felt that *laissez-faire* would give the strained economy of the empire a chance of revival under the favourable conditions of the *pax Romana*, the fact remains that Augustus and his successors limited the task of the State to that of 'night watchman' for the business-man.

The revival of trade and industry was thus carried out under the aegis of private enterprise. Indeed throughout the whole economic field the mines constituted perhaps the only exception to this rule; and although Tiberius (A.D. 14–37) set about bringing these under imperial ownership, their exploitation was often leased to contracting companies or, as at Vipasca in Portugal, carried out by small groups of contractors working their own concessions. Otherwise, *laissez-faire* reigned. Even Egypt, the classic home of state-control, saw some relaxation in the centralization of the economy; and the corn supply, on which Rome

1. Cf. J. B. Bury, *Quart. Rev.* CXCII, 1900, 147.
2. F. M. Heichelheim, *Wirtschaftsgeschichte des Altertums*, Vol. I, Leiden, 1938, p. 674.

depended for her existence, was secured by private shipowners, *navicularii*, who were offered special concessions if they undertook government work. The State, it is true, had an indirect interest in trade, in so much as it drew taxes on its proceeds. Frontier dues, *octrois*, and tolls were a useful source of revenue, which did not hinder trade overmuch; but even the collection of these was leased out to companies. By the building of roads, with milestones, harbour-moles, quays, lighthouses, bridges and canals, the imperial government encouraged the opening-up of new trade routes, and sent Roman soldiers to protect key points. But the big profits went to the individual entrepreneur, and Pliny could remark sarcastically that the very military standards had been corrupted with the promise of perfumes to embark upon the campaigns that conquered the world.[1]

Naturally, one important part of this programme was the provision of a sound coinage; and the golden *aureus*, weighing *c*. $\frac{1}{40}$ of a pound,[2] and first minted in large quantities by Julius Caesar, rapidly became the most important coin in the Empire, and enjoyed a good repute throughout every part of the world which used a money economy. Early imperial *aurei* have been found as far afield as Scandinavia, Siberia, India, Ceylon, South-East Africa and even China—a remarkable commentary on the extent of trade throughout this period.

The different provinces varied considerably in their share of this prosperity. Italy, the heart of the Empire, and the most economically advanced, formed for a time the focal point of the whole Mediterranean area, and enjoyed an especially flourishing trade with the newly opened up provinces of the north and west. Its abundant supplies of fish, meat, fruit, cheese, wood, stone and iron were widely exchanged within the peninsula. Still more important was the organization of the production, with the help of slave labour, of wine and oil on capitalistic lines for export, particularly to the northern and western provinces of the Danube frontier, to Germany, Gaul, Spain and Africa; and with these went the skilled workmanship of the textile factories of Campania and South Italy, the bronzework and glassware of Campania, and the mass produced red-glaze pottery from the kilns of Arretium. The

1. Pliny, *Nat. hist.* xiii, 23.
2. The Roman pound (*libra*) weighed 327.45 grammes or .721 of the pound avoirdupois.

greater part of these goods passed through the town of Aquileia, which thus prospered not only from its native amber industry, but also from the transit trade conducted by such well-known merchant houses as the Barbii and the Statii, who despatched both Italian and overseas commodities to the Danube and to Istria in exchange for slaves, cattle, hides, wax, cheese, honey and other primary commodities, and for Norican wool and iron. Further south, the extent of Italian export trade is reflected in the rich and elaborate homes of the wealthy merchants of Pompeii and Aquileia; and in exchange Italy received luxuries from every part of the Empire and outside it.

To the eastern provinces the *pax Augusta* brought a respite from war and a renewed prosperity. Egypt, the granary of Rome, sustained the population of the capital for four months of each year. The fine marbles of the provinces were shipped overseas, and even the Nile sands went to dust the floors of Roman wrestling-schools. Next to her grain, Egypt's main export commodity was papyrus, which formed virtually the sole source of paper in the ancient world. Under the Empire, as under the Ptolemies (323–30 B.C.), the production of papyrus was a state monopoly; and the desire to make it as profitable as possible led to a practice which has a familiar ring to a generation which has grown accustomed to the paradox of artificially-induced scarcity. Strabo writes of the state-officials in the papyrus-producing areas of the Delta that

certain of those who wish to enhance the revenues adopt the shrewd practice of the Judaeans, which the latter invented in the case of the palm tree; for they refuse to let the papyrus grow in many places and because of the scarcity they set a higher price on it and thus increase the revenues, though they injure the common use of the plant.[1]

From this passage it is clear that in Egypt state monopoly had reached a high peak of organization.

Besides her importance as a source of raw materials, Egypt also produced a wide range of industrial goods. The workshops of Alexandria turned out glass-ware of every type, cheap or expensive, together with sham pearls and precious stones of paste. The textile industry, though organized on the basis of individual craftmanship, produced for mass export; not only were the fine linens, for which Egypt had long been famous, still manufactured, but also special lines of clothing for the natives of Somaliland, just as

1. xvii, 800.

today the mills of Lancashire produce special patterns and qualities for export to India and Ghana. Finally, the metalware of Egypt found a ready sale everywhere; examples have been dug up even in South Russia and India.

Egyptian textiles had a close rival in the woollens, silks and linens of Syria. Here the famous purple-dye, extracted from the murex, gave Syrian products a natural start over all their rivals. Strabo[1] refers to the countless dye-works, especially those at Tyre 'from which the city, while becoming a most unpleasant place to live in, at the same time grew rich'. It was in Syria too, Pliny records,[2] that glass-blowing was invented in the first century of our era. The glass-ware of Ennion of Sidon was renowned far and wide, and specimens of it have been found in Egypt, Cyprus, Italy and South Russia. It is possible that he established a branch at Rome, or perhaps eventually transferred his business there. However, Syria did not depend primarily on its manufactures. An equally important article of trade was furnished by the products of the rich, well-irrigated soil—fine wines, fruits, olives, plums, figs and dates. In a land dependent on the conservation of rainfall, an elaborate system of cisterns, trenches, dams and tunnels ensured outstanding crops in areas which neglect has today rendered uninhabitable. Here trade was taken very seriously. According to the Talmud prayers were offered up—even on the Sabbath—if the price of wine and oil dropped to 60 per cent of its normal market-rate. Syria and Palestine were particularly favourably placed for foreign trade. Antioch with its port Seleuceia-in-Pieria had connections with every part of the Mediterranean, and inherited some of the old Phoenician carrying trade. Syria also profited from her position astride some of the most important caravan routes with the east, which enabled her to maintain trade relations with lands as far afield as India, Siam and China.

Asia Minor also benefited from the transit trade between east and west; and here, even more than in Syria (and in contrast to Egypt), the industrial centres were spread out widely over the whole land. The provinces of this peninsula all show, by their inscriptions, how much they gained from the pax Augusta. Few provinces can have suffered so harshly from the iniquities of Roman economic exploitation under the Republic. The carefully balanced economy of the monarchy of Pergamum had been disrupted by

1. xvi, 757.   2. Nat. hist. xxxvi, 191.

the system of farming out the tax-collecting on five-yearly contracts. The pent-up anger of the provincials had avenged itself with the massacre of a figure variously estimated at 80,000 and 150,000 Italians; and the settlement of Sulla had involved re-enslavement of those who had asserted their freedom, together with massacres and a savage indemnity, which drove the provincials into the hands of the money-lenders, who were often identical with the tax-collectors. Shortly afterwards the province had suffered severely from the ravages of the pirates, a plague endemic around the shores of Cilicia, which had grown through the supine attitude of the Senate and the connivance of the Italian slavers. Over four hundred towns and islands had fallen into their hands before the Senate was roused to send out Pompey to round them up. Meanwhile the collecting of the taxes remained in the hands of the tax-farmers until the time of Caesar.

To this unhappy area the Empire brought a relief and prosperity which is reflected in the inscriptions. Among the exports were wine, raisins, dried figs, honey, truffles, cheese, salted tunny-fish, timber, drugs, various metals and a wide range of marbles and precious stones. Above all, Asia Minor joined Egypt and Syria in the world textile market; fine woollens from the famous breeds of Miletus, and the glossy black wool of Laodiceia, Coan silks, Lydian embroideries and tapestries, goat's hair jackets from Cilicia, linen from Tarsus, and Anatolian rugs and carpets were famous all over the Roman world. Interesting too is the structure of this industry. Though we meet serfs and tenants on the land, the industrial hand is generally a free man—a significant contrast to Italy where, as we shall see, industry made widespread use of slave labour.

To these areas Greece provides an unhappy contrast. The battlefield of Roman armies from the time of the wars against Philip V of Macedon, in the late third and early second century B.C., to those against Mithridates of Pontus in the first, Greece had long since sunk to a shadow of her ancient self. Writing in the second century B.C., Polybius describes the ruin of his country, the fall in the birthrate 'owing to which cities have become deserted and the land has ceased to bear fruit';[1] and subsequently the Mithridatic Wars of the first century dealt the country further blows. How far the economic decay had penetrated by the time

1. *Hist.* xxxvi, 17.

of the Principate is not easy to determine. But the literary authorities—perhaps not without rhetorical over-statement—present a dismal picture. Servius Sulpicius writing to Cicero speaks of Aegina, Megara, Corinth and the Piraeus as *oppidum cadavera*, corpses of cities; and the younger Seneca suggests that the very foundations of some Achaean cities had vanished. In about A.D. 100 Dio Chrysostom writes of a (perhaps imaginary) Euboean town, which had allowed two-thirds of its land to go to wilderness. Overdrawn though such pictures may perhaps be, they suggest that the recovery under the *pax Augusta* was not sufficient to restore Greek prosperity. Greece still exported oil (from Attica) and wine (from Chios and Lesbos), together with livestock, and honey and marbles from Hymettus; but like Italy, which was also organized for export, she had to bring in her basic corn from abroad. In general, the picture presented by the writers of the Empire, and by the findings of archaeology, is one of economic weakness, and of extremes of wealth and poverty combined with bad finance in the cities. The effects of the *pax Augusta* were not negligible: but they were less remarkable than in most provinces, since the decay was already far advanced.

When one turns to the western provinces, which had been more recently assimilated into the system of world trade, the impression is more striking. For here it is a question not merely of restoring prosperity, but of positively creating streams of new life. Gallia Narbonensis—Provence and Languedoc—had long been a second Italy, with a prosperity based on the intensive cultivation of vines and olives. Now northern Gaul entered the field of trade, and its wide, fertile cornlands helped to provision the capital, while the products of its stock-farms were regularly imported into Italy. Timber too was an important export. Lumbermen working in the forests which still covered much of the country built rafts and so floated their logs down the broad rivers of France for eventual export to Italy and Rome, where they furnished fuel for between eight and nine hundred public baths. But the significant feature in the economy of Gaul during the early Empire is the phenomenal growth and power of its industries, which rapidly became serious competitors on the world market. Not only its textiles—woollens and linens, manufactured mainly by domestic industry from the plentiful local supplies of wool and flax—but also its pottery acquired a dominating position and it is worth noting that among the finds at Pompeii was a case of pottery from central Gaul, unopened at the time of the catastrophe. Thus by A.D. 79 Gaul had begun to capture the Italian market from the home producer.

In metal work too great strides were made. Tin-plating of bronze was a Gallic invention, and silver-plating was practised in Alesia before the Roman conquest; later the brass-ware of the Ardennes to some extent ousted bronze, and the glass of Arles and Lyons, and afterwards Cologne, was famous throughout the west. Much of the stimulus for this movement came from the influx of north Italians and Romans into Gaul. The passes had now been rendered safe and the Alpine tribes pacified; and if we can believe Cicero, towards the end of the Republic Gaul was full of Roman citizens, traders and tax-collectors, who, he suggests, between them controlled most of its economy.[1]

Britain, which was only included in the Empire after Claudius's invasion in A.D. 43, remained for many years a producer of raw materials, buying its made-up goods—wine, oil, bronze-ware, pottery and glass—from the older lands, and exporting corn, cattle and minerals—gold, silver, iron, tin and lead—hides, hounds and, above all, slaves in exchange. The three legions and their auxiliaries stationed in the island demanded the import of many commodities which must at first have been strange to the native inhabitants; but in addition they satisfied many of their needs from legionary industries, such as the army kilns at Holt in Denbighshire, which supplemented the imported red-ware pottery. Britain was a relatively backward area: yet even this remote province had become virtually self-sufficient in all but wine and oil by the end of the first century of our era. Spain, too, had its important mines in the Sierra Morena and Galicia. Though public property in the second century B.C., they had come into private hands when Strabo described them during the Principate of Augustus; from the time of Tiberius onwards, however, they seem once more to have been imperial property, and to have been worked either by contracting companies or directly under imperial officials. It has been estimated that the silver mines of New Carthage alone had a yearly output of some eight and a third tons. But in addition Spain exported a variety of products, both agricultural and industrial. From Andalusia in the south came corn,

1. Cicero, pro Fonteio, 11–12.

wine, olive oil, wax, honey, pitch, dyestuffs, and the famous pickled fish and fish-sauce; and from other parts of Spain esparto-grass (for cords), linen yarns and fabrics, woollens, and articles of wrought steel. But of all these commodities olive oil and wine occupied a pre-eminent place. Monte Testaccio, a vast mound of broken potsherds beside the Tiber emporium at Rome, 140 feet high and 3,000 feet in circumference, has been shown to consist of the fragments of about forty million jars from Spain, each of which originally held approximately eleven gallons of wine or oil. Here is a concrete and staggering proof of the success of the Spanish wine and oil producers in capturing the Roman market under the early Empire. Altogether the peninsula enjoyed great prosperity; its cities grew in number and size, and with these the trading classes. According to Strabo, Gades (Cadiz) was the second city of the Empire, the number of its capitalists being equalled in Patavium alone.

The remaining western provinces, Sicily and Africa, were, like Egypt, devoted to the production and export of corn. Without a regular flow of some seventeen million bushels of corn a year (of which Egypt is said to have furnished five, Africa ten, and Sicily perhaps two) Rome could not exist; and the organization of the corn traffic under a government department, which leased out the shipping to private contractors, will be discussed below. In addition Sicily produced livestock. But as the oldest Roman province, it had less to gain than Spain, Gaul and Britain from the Augustan peace, and its economy was considerably re-tarded by the existence of large estates owned by senators living at Rome. Neither here nor in Africa was industry on a significant scale; indeed African woollens were the only industrial commodity to win an international reputation. Second in importance only to corn was the African export of olive oil; and in addition the province grew all kinds of other fruit produce—palms, figs, pomegranates—as well as vines and leguminous plants. From Mauretania came citron-wood, precious stones, pearls and ivory, and wild beasts for the Roman circus. Finally, to complete this rapid survey, the northern frontier provinces, corresponding to modern Switzerland, Tyrol and the Danube States, were a source of minerals, and did an extensive trade through Aquileia, which had the same relation to these areas as Trieste has today.

Such details, of which space limits us to a bare selection,

combine to present a picture of a world knit together, to a degree
hitherto unknown, by the intensive exchange of all types of
primary commodities and manufactured articles, including the
four fundamental articles of trade—grain, wine, oil and slaves.
This trade was aided by a system of communications of an
efficiency never reached again for some 1200 years after the fall of
Rome. Throughout the whole of the Empire and outside it too,
in such countries as Parthia, there was a well-organized network
of rivers, military roads connecting the frontier posts, the legionary centres, the provincial capitals and Rome itself, and such
canals as that from the Rhine to the North Sea, or from the Red
Sea to the Nile. Fairs and markets furthered cultural as well as
economic interchange. There were inns and charted water-
supplies, river and sea flotillas affording police protection, and a
police force on land to protect the trader from brigandage, as
far east as India. Finally, both the Roman and Parthian Empires
ran a state postal-service, covering up to forty miles a day.

The important far-eastern trade followed the caravan routes
of central Asia, which reached the Mediterranean by way of
Arabia and the rock-city of Petra, or up the Euphrates and so via
Palmyra to Damascus; and the port of Alexandria Charax at the
mouth of the Tigris, where goods were shipped from India, was
the terminus of many routes from the Mediterranean, Armenia,
and Asia Minor. But there is some evidence that to avoid en-
riching Parthia the Romans encouraged a more northerly route,
via the Oxus, the Caspian and the Caucasus, debouching on the
shores of the Black Sea. After the discovery of the monsoons by
Hippalus, a Greek sea-captain, about 100 B.C., it became possible
to leave Puteoli with the Egyptian corn-boats in May and, continuing by Nile-craft and caravan to the Red Sea, to sail direct
to the coast of Malabar, arriving with good winds some sixteen
weeks after leaving Italy; and by using the north-eastern monsoon
the following November or December one might complete the
round trip inside a year—so close, adds Pliny, had India been
brought by greed![1] Nor was India linked with Rome merely by
the carrying trade. Recent excavations on the Coromandel coast
at Arikamedu have revealed the remains of a Roman trading
station dating from the first century of our era. The tonnage of
vessels engaged in this commerce is a subject of controversy; but

1. *Nat. hist.* vi, 101f.

the most recent studies suggest that the ships of the crack Alexandrian corn fleet carried 1,200 to 1,300 tons of grain, and that ordinary freighters reached 340 tons.[1]

The position of the city of Rome inside this system was somewhat peculiar, and due to the historical development of the late republic. The acquisition of a profitable eastern empire in the second century B.C. had been paid for with the ruin of Italian agriculture. The sixteen years' war with Hannibal in Italy (218–202 B.C.) had already devastated the Italian countryside. In the course of the war South Italy had gone over to the enemy, a defection which the Romans punished with the destruction of some four hundred villages. Hannibal was driven in turn to a similar policy, and thus large parts of Italy were made desolate. After the war confiscations and the letting out of depopulated territory, especially in the south, for grazing, changed the face of the countryside. Meanwhile the small farmer had been ruined. On his return from the legions to a burnt-out farmstead, he had neither the heart nor the money to recommence farming, and often enough sold his holding to the local landowner or some speculator from the capital. Citizen-farmers made way for slave-worked *latifundia*, and a dispossessed peasantry drifted to Rome, there to play the part of potential troublemaker in the conflicts between the ruling oligarchy and *populares* like Marius and Caesar, who were playing for personal power. Meanwhile the rich trafficked in real estate, and the greatest fortunes of the second century probably sprang from this source.

To some extent this movement was checked during the next century. Grants of land were made on various occasions from the time of Tiberius Gracchus (133 B.C.) onwards, and they were used to settle many labourers on farms; the trend towards city pauperism, especially in the case of retired veterans, was halted by Sulla, and later by Caesar, Octavian and Antony. Indeed it has been calculated that Antony and Octavian (if we include Octavian's

1. Des Noëttes, *De la marine antique à la marine moderne* (1935), p. 70, argued that Roman ships were in the main quite small craft of less than 100 tons; for the higher and more convincing figures see L. Casson, *The Ancient Mariners* (London, 1954), 215; *Studi in onore di A. Calderini e R. Paribeni*, 1 (Milan, 1956), 231–8.

land assignments after he became Augustus) between them settled 300,000 soldiers on the land—though indeed this was not all clear gain, since many received plots whose owners had been dispossessed and driven overseas. It is certainly true that *latifundia* do not appear to be the typical form of holding during the last century of the Republic and first century of the Principate; if they made any headway at this time it was in the hill country rather than in the fertile valleys.

However, despite the partial success of this movement towards small-holdings, it made little impression on the population of Rome. Here the mob, the nominal rulers of the Empire, were increasingly kept quiet with gifts of cheap corn and the provision of elaborate and expensive shows by the politicians who courted their favour; and at the other end of the scale, these same politicians found it indispensable to amass a fortune sufficient for these manoeuvres during the years they spent abroad, governing a province in the service of the State. The fantastic figures of the loot taken by Julius Caesar—25,000,000 sesterces in Spain, captives worth 100,000,000 denarii from Gaul,[1] and so much gold that, sold on the market, it brought down the price by a sixth—may furnish 'the ugliest example in Roman history of provincial looting for personal gain';[2] but they are only different in quantity from the gains of dozens of Caesar's fellow governors and rival generals.

Thus in one way or another the provinces found themselves obliged to shoulder the whole burden of an extravagant oligarchy and an unnaturally swollen and degraded populace, the two constituents into which a once homogeneous mass of peasant-soldiers had been split up by the catalytic action of war and imperial conquest; and the feelings of the provincials were not to be concealed. Cicero writes:

Words cannot express, gentlemen, how bitterly hated we are among foreign nations because of the wanton and outrageous conduct of the men whom in recent years we have sent to govern them. For in those countries what temple do you suppose has been held sacred by our officers, what state inviolable, what home sufficiently guarded by its closed doors? Why, they

1. There were four sesterces (*sestertii*) to the *denarius* and under Augustus the *denarius* weighed $\frac{1}{84}$ of a Roman pound. 25 *denarii* went to one *aureus*.
2. T. Frank, *Economic Survey of Ancient Rome*, 1, 325.

look about for rich and flourishing cities that they may find an occasion for
a war against them to satisfy their lust for plunder.[1]

The establishment of the Principate changed the form, but not
the fact of this flow of wealth from the provinces to the leech-like
city at the heart of the Empire. The vast imperial estates in Egypt,
inherited from the Ptolemies, represented a constant subsidy
flowing in to the centre; and we have already seen how the corn
of Egypt, Africa, Gaul and Sicily was imported to maintain the
people of Rome. This raises the question of the balance of trade.
How far did Rome (and by implication Italy) pay for its imports
of corn and luxuries with Roman and Italian exports? Strabo[2] has
a picture of ships returning empty to Egypt from Puteoli, which
was chiefly an exporting harbour, serving the rich areas of
Campania; and though this in itself may be inconclusive, since
Italy exported mainly to the north and the west, Pliny asserts[3]
that India, China and Arabia took an annual sum of 100 million
sesterces from the Empire, a statement confirmed by the discovery of numerous Roman *aurei* all over India, and even in
Ceylon and China. Now the products of the east were mainly
luxuries such as found their normal market in Rome—dancing
girls, parrots, ebony, ivory, pearls and precious stones, spices, silks
and drugs—and it is a fair assumption that the coins going east were
in payment for goods coming to the capital.

This far eastern demand for Roman *aurei* has been explained
as a tribute to the excellence and reliability of that coin. But
perhaps an equally valid reason is that difficulties of transport and
the structure of the far-eastern societies made it impossible to
balance the cost of these luxuries with the products of mass industry or agriculture. Consequently, despite such commerce as is
implied by the post at Arikamedu, the eastern trade involved a
constant drain of metal from the Empire, and this proved an
important factor in the developments we shall shortly consider.

Meanwhile, notwithstanding the phenomenal expansion of trade
and industry, the vast majority of people inside the Empire still
gained their livelihood from the soil. Agriculture remained

1. Cicero, *pro lege Manilia*, 65.   2. xvii, 793.   3. *Nat. hist.* xii, 84.

Ostia houses. Restoration (by I. Gismondi) of the 'Casa dei Dipinti' at Ostia, showing the inner court of this large apartment-house.

The Pont du Gard, which carried the water supply of Nîmes over the Gardon near Remoulins, was probably built under Augustus; it is 273 metres long and 49 metres high.

Spanish Miners. Bas-relief from Linares in Spain, showing miners descending a gallery to a pit, and carrying various implements. Silver and lead were mined at Linares (ancient Castulo).

Terra sigillata.
A specimen
manufactured at
Lezoux and now in
the British Museum.

throughout antiquity the most usual and most typical economic activity, and land the most important form of wealth. But now the agricultural science of Greece was applied to increase its productivity. Farms supplying the market were established all over the new western provinces. In A.D. 33 Tiberius set a fashion to later emperors by a loan of 100 million sesterces to relieve an agricultural crisis. Under such stimuli and the favourable conditions of peace, well-appointed villas sprang up all over the areas under Roman control, with mosaic pavements and, where the climate demanded it, hypocausts to provide central heating.

In this way the culture of Greece and Rome began to penetrate even the countryside of Spain and Britain. The consolidation of world trade inevitably led to an exchange of experiences between the various peoples and individuals of the Empire, a breaking down of parochialism, and a general levelling up of manners and ways of behaviour. Not the least part in this process was contributed by the permanent army of from 250,000 to 300,000 men, which stood guard along the 4,000 mile frontier of the north and east, the bulwark against the barbarians without. In Augustus's disposition, out of a total of twenty-five legions, eight were stationed along the Rhine, seven in the Danubian lands of Pannonia, Dalmatia and Illyria, four in Syria to watch the Parthians, two in Egypt, one in Numidia to ward off the nomads of the desert, and three in Spain. Based on long-term enlistment by volunteers, and each with a permanent number and distinctive title, the legions developed regimental histories and traditions; and though the original plan of recruiting for the legions only in Italy had broken down (largely from financial reasons) as early as Tiberius (A.D. 14–37), so that provincial volunteers were accepted, and though from the outset the auxiliary troops were raised from non-citizens in the less cultured parts—northern Gaul, the Spanish plateau, Thrace, Batavia and the like—the service itself proved an education and a force for Romanization. Moreover, after it became clear from the civil war of A.D. 69 how dangerous native troops might prove when serving under native officers in their own country, Vespasian adopted the policy of posting auxiliaries to areas other than that of their birth, and this movement of troops in itself acted as a constant leavening of the mass. Today the visitor to Housesteads Camp on the Roman Wall in Northumberland can read the dedication of Tungrian soldiers (from Belgium) to their Teutonic gods, and see concrete evidence of what this interchange of experience meant in the life of the Empire.

This then was the Empire at its height. And we are now face to face with our problem. What we must ask is: Why within a hundred years did this vigorous and complicated structure cease to operate as a going concern? Why has there been, not a straight upward line of progress from the time of Hadrian to the twentieth century, but instead the familiar sequence of decay, middle ages, renaissance and modern world?

To some historians it has seemed that the whole tragedy might have been avoided if some trivial error had not been committed: if only Julius Caesar could have been murdered a little later (or a little sooner, according to one's particular estimate of Caesar's role), if only Trajan had not extended the Empire a little too far (or, alternatively, if only Hadrian had not promptly re-established the old frontiers), all might have been well and the catastrophe averted. Another school, which will have nothing to do with a scheme of causation which smacks so much of chance, locates the fatal factor virtually outside man's control, in the deterioration of the climate (in accordance with certain postulated cycles), in the spread of plague or malaria, in the exhaustion of the soil or in a general decline in the population from about A.D. 150 onwards, leading to a chronic shortage of manpower. Others reply reasserting the collective guilt of the inhabitants of the empire, who either let themselves be corrupted by vice, or, by race-suicide, dysgenic breeding or some other biological crime, caused a permanent deterioration in the Roman stock.

Others again have urged that constant warfare brought about the destruction of the best stock of the Empire; that the fault was political—a failure to reconcile empire and self-government, or to prevent power falling into the hands of the indispensable army; or else that a combination of social and political errors was at the root of the trouble, that Rome fell because of class-war, because she allowed free enterprise to deteriorate into bureaucratic centralism, because of high taxation or the use of slave-labour, or because of the exclusiveness of ancient culture, viewed in relation to the vast peasant masses of the Empire. Finally, within the last twenty years, and perhaps not uninfluenced by recent happenings, the theory has been advanced that the crisis was already past, and that Rome was well on the way to rebuilding a new society, when she fell before the weapons of barbarism. 'Roman civilization did not die a natural death: it was murdered!'[1]

We cannot here attempt a complete survey of answers to a problem which so many have tried to solve; but the above form a representative selection. Some may be dismissed at once. Thus the theories of land exhaustion ignore Egypt, where the Nile renews the land annually, yet Egypt provides one of our earliest examples of depopulation and peasants in flight. The Great Plague of A.D. 167 had its successors: the epidemic which spread from Ethiopia in A.D. 250, under the emperor Decius, lasted for fifteen years and reached every part of the Empire. But there is no evidence that it had permanent results; and malaria, which others regard as the arch-enemy, has never been more than a local problem in the Mediterranean. Nor will any climatic evidence so far put forward—certainly not evidence drawn from the big trees of California on which one scholar has based far-reaching conclusions—fit, still less explain, the ups and downs of Graeco-Roman civilization. Vice too, is scarcely a feasible explanation; the pages of Tacitus and Suetonius should not mislead us into imagining that luxury and profligate living ever affected more than a minority. The charge of racial deterioration really begs the question; for although there was a very considerable racial intermixture both at Rome and elsewhere (though perhaps less than arguments based on the names to be found on sepulchral inscriptions suggest), it is difficult to single out any one of the races involved as specifically dysgenic. The theory that the third century emperors deliberately exterminated the most outstanding citizens, which was advanced by a great German historian, will not stand up to detailed examination, for the centuries both before and after Diocletian saw some of the most outstanding figures the world has ever known governing the Empire from Rome and Constantinople or active in the organization of the Christian Church. Finally the theory of a renascent civilization assassinated by the malice of German hordes acting in conjunction with traitors within the gates poses as many questions as it answers. In the past the Empire had faced barbarian invasions

1. A. Piganiol, *L'Empire chrétien* (325–95), 422.

successfully: why was it now unequal to the task? No one can deny that the *coup de grâce* came from without: but the development of the barbarian forces themselves was not a process occurring in isolation from the Empire.

In short, many of these alleged reasons may be eliminated at the outset. But they leave behind a solid core of some half a dozen causes, mainly of a political and social-political character; and if these are compared, it will be clear that they embrace many of the phenomena which are closely associated with the decline of the Empire. The problem is to separate symptom from cause. Family limitation, the failure to maintain self-government, class-war, a military usurpation of power, bureaucratic centralism, an intolerable burden of taxation, a civilization of vast extent but insufficient depth, slave-labour—all these are part of the story of what was wrong; but none *alone* is enough to explain the fall of Rome. Taken together, however, they suggest that our bird's-eye view of the early Empire may have been misleading; therefore we must penetrate behind the veil of Antonine prosperity and try, with the help of the new tools provided by modern research, to isolate some of the tendencies which were developing within the fabric of this apparently blessed society.

NOTES FOR FURTHER READING

The economic background of the early Empire is dealt with by F. Oertel, *Cambridge Ancient History*, Vol. X, 1934, pp. 382–424, 'The economic unification of the Mediterranean region'. The classic study of this question is Rostovtzeff's work, mentioned in the notes following Chapter I; he has since covered the earlier period in the three splendidly illustrated volumes of his *Social and Economic History of the Hellenistic World*, Oxford, 1941. Indispensable too, for detailed work, is T. Frank's *Economic Survey of Ancient Rome*, Vols. I–V, Baltimore, 1933–40; and readers of German will find much good material in F. M. Heichelheim, *Wirtschaftsgeschichte des Altertums* (2 vols.; Leiden, 1938) of which an English version is now appearing, *An Ancient Economic History*, Leiden, 1958. Useful too are the outspoken writings of W. E. Heitland, viz. *Agricola*, Cambridge, 1921, a study of the land question in the ancient world; the three pamphlets mentioned on p. 113, n. 1; and his chapter on agriculture in *The Legacy of Rome*, Oxford, 1928, a book well worth general perusal for its account of the Roman heritage and how it was transmitted in various fields. Two valuable books on the commerce of the Empire are E. H. Warmington, *The Commerce between the Roman*

Empire and India, Cambridge, 1928, and M. P. Charlesworth, *Trade Routes of the Roman Empire*, Cambridge, 1924, both reliable and fascinating surveys. For a recent argument that the main factor in the decline of Rome was man-power shortage see A. E. R. Boak, *Manpower Shortage and the Fall of the Roman Empire in the West*, Ann Arbor, 1955; in an important review (*Journ. Rom. Stud.*, 1958, pp. 156–64) M. I. Finley shows that this was a created shortage, the result largely of government demands, and so a symptom rather than a cause.

3

TRENDS IN THE EMPIRE OF
THE SECOND CENTURY A.D.

THE *pax Augusta* brought prosperity to a wide area of the earth's surface; but it completely failed to release new productive forces. As in the century after Alexander's death in 323 B.C.—a century in many ways comparable to the early Empire—the step to industrialization and the factory was never taken. Indeed, except for a few new devices such as the mill wheel, which was probably invented in the first century after Christ, but never became really popular until after the fall of the Western Empire, or the invention of valved bellows in the fourth century of our era, which for the first time made complete smelting possible, the level of technique inside the Roman Empire never surpassed that already reached in Alexandria. Nor was this due to any special Roman foible; on the contrary it continued the classical tradition of the Alexandrines, who could find no better use for many of their mechanical devices than to impress the ignorant congregations in the Egyptian temples and to bolster up their religion with sham miracles. For the origins of this tradition one must go back to the Greek city-state.

From its outset classical civilization inherited a low level of technical skill, judged by the part Greece and Rome were destined to play in history. The Greek tribes settled in a poor and rocky land; only by incessant labour could Hesiod wring a livelihood from the soil of Boeotia. Consequently, the leisure which was to bring forth the Ionian Renaissance and the fine flower of Periclean Athens could only be purchased at a price. For the conception of democracy—that a people shall as a whole take the responsibility for its own destiny—we are in permanent debt to fifth century Athens. But it is to modern eyes paradoxical that ancient democracy, and nowhere more than in Athens itself, was wedded to imperialism. The very temples on the Athenian Acropolis, which still inspire our wonder and admiration, were built out of the tribute of subject cities. Originally united in a confederacy of mutual defence against Persia, after the glories of Salamis and Plataea had temporarily inspired them to sink their inveterate particularism for the common good of Greece, these cities had quickly been degraded to the level of subjects, and blockaded and reduced if they attempted to resist or secede. In return for nominal protection against Persia which was no longer a serious danger and real protection against the machinations of their own oligarchic parties they were henceforth obliged to subsidize the cultural life of their masters.

The Athenians mulcted both their subject-allies and their resident aliens; nor had their slaves and women-folk any share in the full life of the city-state. Nevertheless one must not exaggerate the evil of slavery at this stage. The Athenian domestic slave was not ill-treated: indeed if one can believe a contemporary, though prejudiced witness, he was often hard to distinguish from his master. Moreover the Athenians themselves in the main lived frugally, simple in their private lives and magnificent in their communal enterprises. What one can say with justice is that the evil seeds were there; and eventually imperialism brought its nemesis, the fall of Athens as a great power and in due course the end of democracy. At Rome the extremes were greater. There democracy was never achieved. The wealth of the late Republic was built up, as we saw, on the sweat of the provinces, the loot of many wars, and the sufferings of countless slaves enduring abject misery on the plantations of aristocratic landowners, resident in Rome. This relationship of absentee landlord and plantation slave reproduced in an accentuated form that contrast which underlay ancient civilization, between the leisured class of the city and the multitude labouring to support it on the land—a contrast which evoked Rostovtzeff's famous criticism of the cities of the Empire as 'hives of drones'.

This antithesis was no new thing; like the low level of classical technique, it had been characteristic of the ancient civilizations which sprang up in the river valleys of Egypt, Mesopotamia and the Punjab round about the third millenium B.C. Common to the east too was the institution of slavery, which spread from the home to the mine and the plantation, to become the basis of Greek and Roman civilization, a cancer in the flesh of society which grew with society itself. Slavery was never effectively challenged. Aristotle (384–322 B.C.), although clearly among the world's most acute philosophers and students of political science, laid it down as axiomatic that

from the hour of their birth some are marked out for subjection, others for rule[1]; ... the art of war is a natural art of acquisition, for it includes hunting, an art which we ought to practise against wild beasts and against men who, though intended by nature to be governed, will not submit; for war of such a kind is naturally just.[2]

It is perhaps not strange that a philosopher who so faithfully reflects the practice of his own society in framing his definition of a just war should also have sought to demonstrate the natural inferiority of woman to man.

After Aristotle another school of philosophers arose, the Stoics, who for a short time asserted the equality of slaves and free men; but they never passed from this to the obvious conclusion that slavery should be abolished. Very soon they too lapsed back into the easier Aristotelian view. Meanwhile slavery was spreading both geographically and in the number of human beings which it enveloped in its folds. The wars of Alexander's successors and of the Roman republic brought a constantly increasing supply; especially on the plantations and sheep ranches and in the mines they formed an indispensable source of labour. At Rome 'Sardinians for sale—each more scoundrelly than the next' was a popular proverb for anything in cheap supply after 177 B.C., when Ti. Sempronius Gracchus, the father of the reformers, boasted of 80,000 Sardinians slain or taken prisoner. Ten years later 150,000 Epirotes were enslaved by the Senate's orders; and the total number of captives taken in half a century of constant warfare has been estimated at a quarter of a million. For the later years of the second century B.C. Strabo has left us a highly coloured picture of the infamous slave market of Delos (xiv, 668):

the island could admit and send away tens of thousands of slaves in the same day.... The cause of this was the fact that the Romans, having become rich after the destruction of Carthage and Corinth (146 B.C.), used many slaves; and the pirates, seeing the easy profit therein, bloomed forth in great numbers, themselves not only going in quest of booty, but also trafficking in slaves.

It was this slavery at the root of society which in some degree controlled the pattern of classical civilization. For it split up every

1. *Politics*, i, 5, 2. 1254a.   2. *Ibid.* i, 5, 8. 1256b.

community into two kinds of human beings—the free man and the slave; and it ensured that those who did the basic work of society should not be those to benefit from it. The natural outcome was that the slave lacked the incentive to master and improve the technique of the work he was doing. Equally disastrous was the effect upon the slave owners themselves. Because it became normal to associate manual labour with slaves, Greek culture tended to draw a line between the things of the hand and the things of the mind. In the *Republic*, Plato (*c.* 427–347 B.C.) pictured a utopian community divided into three sharply differentiated classes, endowed each with some imaginary 'metallic' quality—Guardians with a golden cast of mind, to govern; Auxiliaries with an admixture of silver, to fight and police the State; and finally Workers, sharing in the base metals, to do the work of society and to obey. It seems likely—though the matter is disputed—that Plato envisaged some degree of transfer between the three groups for those born into the 'wrong' section; but this provision does not greatly alter the picture and the significance of Plato's approach to the problem of building the just city. Aristotle, with an equal contempt for manual work, writes:

Doubtless in ancient times the artisan class were slaves or foreigners, and therefore the majority of them are so now. The best form of state will not admit them to citizenship.[1]

Certainly the good man . . . and the good citizen ought not to learn the crafts of inferiors except for their own occasional use; if they habitually practise these, there will cease to be a distinction between master and slave.[2]

The Roman attitude varied no whit from this; indeed Greek thought merely served to reinforce the traditional prejudices of a landed aristocracy. Cicero's formulation deserves to be quoted in full. He writes:[3]

Public opinion divides the trades and professions into the liberal and the vulgar. We condemn the odious occupation of the collector of customs and the usurer, and the base and menial work of unskilled labourers; for the very wages the labourer receives are a badge of slavery. Equally contemptible is the business of the retail dealer; for he cannot succeed unless he is dishonest, and dishonesty is the most shameful thing in the world. The work of the mechanic is also degrading; there is nothing noble about a workshop. The least respectable of all trades are those which minister to pleasure, as Terence tells us,

1. *Politics*, iii, 5, 3. 1278a.   2. *Ibid.* iii, 4, 13. 1277b.
3. *De officiis*, i, 150–51.

'fishmongers, butchers, cooks, sausage-makers'. Add to these, if you like, perfumers, dancers, and the actors of the gaming-house. But the learned professions, such as medicine, architecture and the higher education, from which society derives the greatest benefit, are considered honourable occupations for those to whose social position they are appropriate. Business on a small scale is despicable; but if it is extensive and imports commodities in large quantities from all over the world and distributes them honestly, it is not so very discreditable; nay, if the merchant, satiated, or rather, satisfied, with the fortune he has made, retires from the harbour and steps into an estate, as once he returned to harbour from the sea, he deserves, I think, the highest respect. But of all the sources of wealth farming is the best, the most able, the most profitable, the most noble.

There was nothing novel in all this. A hundred years earlier the elder Cato had written:

I consider the merchant on the seas an energetic man and well occupied in increasing his estate, but his is a business full of dangers and at times disastrous. From the farm come the bravest men and the most energetic soldiers; the gains of the farmers are the most respectable and the most certain, and awaken least envy. Those who are occupied in farming are least given to unseemly thoughts.[1]

The character of these unseemly thoughts may be guessed at if one bears in mind that government at Rome was in the hands of an aristocratic clique whose wealth was derived from land, and which was debarred by a special law (which originally aroused great opposition) from practising commerce. This caste was the natural opponent of any economic improvement which challenged its own position. After the conquest of Macedonia in 168 B.C. it closed down the Macedonian mines lest they should strengthen the commercial elements which would have worked them; and once current needs could be met from the Spanish mines, the Senate practically stopped mining in Italy.

This maintained Senatorial authority beyond challenge: but it also checked the economic expansion which might have restored the balance in the country.[2]

It was this landed class which peopled the countryside of Italy and Sicily with the slave gangs which later threatened Rome's very existence in the revolt of Spartacus, in which between 60,000 and 120,000 slaves kept the regular legions of the Republic at bay

1. Cato, de agricultura, praef. 4.
2. A. H. McDonald, The Rise of Roman Imperialism, Sydney, 1940, p. 12.

for two years (73–71 B.C.). Meanwhile the towns and cities were filling up with eastern slaves, who not only undertook all kinds of manual work, but also acted as teachers, doctors, architects and professional men. The consequence was that among the ruling class at Rome these activities were ill thought of. Here too Rome followed the city-state, rather than the Hellenistic kingdoms where the attitude was frequently more liberal. 'The meaner sort of mechanic has a special and separate slavery', wrote Aristotle;[1] and similarly the Romans despised the free artisan as one doing work proper to a slave. Thus the atmosphere was wholly unfavourable to technical progress in a field for which men of consequence had nothing but contempt. When labour is cheap and worthless, why conserve it? So the classical world perpetuated that technical retardation which had been one of the most paradoxical features of the civilizations of the Nile and Euphrates—paradoxical because it was thanks to a unique crop of technical inventions—the plough, the wheeled cart, the sailing boat, the solar calendar, the smelting of copper ores, the use of the power of oxen and the harnessing of the winds with sails—that these civilizations had come into being. In both instances the cause of retardation was the same—the bisection of society into classes with contrary interests.

Economically, this division of society ensured that the vast masses of the empire tasted few of the fruits of their labour; and this meant a permanently restricted internal market. Because wealth was concentrated at the top, the body of society suffered from chronic under-consumption. It has been calculated that it was possible in the second century B.C. to hire out a slave at 180 *denarii* per annum and make a slight profit. Clearly free labour could not hope to earn very much more than this so long as slaves were plentiful: and there is independent evidence that a labourer did in fact earn about 300 *denarii* per annum—a figure which represents an extremely meagre subsistence for himself, his wife, and his family, and one which allows no margin for the purchase of luxuries. Accordingly industry had to seek its market either in the limited circle of the middle and upper class, together with the army (which therefore had considerable economic significance), or else outside the Empire, where of course there were even fewer markets for mass-produced goods. Consequently,

1. *Politics*, i, 13, 13. 1260a.

the economic basis for industrialization was not to hand. The expansion of the Empire brought new markets, which staved off the problem for a time; but, as we shall see, the effects of this expansion were soon cancelled out—for Italian producers—by the decentralization of production, and were in any case never radical enough to carry a large-scale industry, using all the resources of advanced technique and advanced forms of power. But so long as this was lacking, production costs remained approximately equal all over the Empire, and in consequence trade remained local and tied to the prosperity of its area. This perhaps reduced the possibility of large-scale economic crises; but it allowed glut and scarcity to exist simultaneously, with great fluctuation of price, even in different parts of the same province, and provided no resilience for tiding over the local crisis under an economy in which everything depended ultimately on the success or failure of the local crop.

This lack of a satisfactory market among the masses was not compensated by the tremendous fortunes which were accumulated, especially during the first century B.C. by such political leaders as Marius, Sulla, Pompey and Caesar. The loot of wars—sometimes provoked, Cicero suggested (above, pp.33–4), for that very purpose—the exploitation of the provincials, and the sordid profits of the proscriptions, with their sales of confiscated property, and half-concealed usury, together resulted in the amassing of wealth on a fantastic scale. But these sums were mostly squandered in ostentatious but unproductive luxury.

On the other hand, because of the social structure, Greece and Rome never even considered the possibility of catering for the proletariat and peasantry, and so creating a deeper, instead of a wider, market. What expansion the Empire brought proves on closer examination to be a matter of greater extension, not of greater depth. The *pax Augusta* removed many handicaps and much wastage; goods circulated with greater ease and over wider areas. But there was no qualitative change in the nature of classical economy. In one field alone there were notable technical achievements—in that of building and engineering, where the Hellenistic Age had already given a lead, under the stimulus of interstate warfare; but even here the Romans were concerned with the amplifying and application of old processes rather than with the creation of new. Thus behind the rosy hues of Gibbon's picture of a prosperous Antonine world we are now in a position to detect at least one notable weakness—the almost complete stagnation of technique.

It has been suggested above that in the long run the expansion of the Roman Empire could bring only a temporary fillip to its economy. The reason why this was so deserves special attention, for it underlines a factor of some importance for our central problem. Modern investigation has revealed in the Roman Empire the operation of an economic law which finds its application equally in our own society—the centrifugal tendency of industry to export itself instead of its products, and of trades to migrate from the older areas of the economy to the new.

The operation of this law was felt with full force in Great Britain when India began to satisfy its own needs with cotton manufactured in Bombay; and the lesson was underlined by mass unemployment in the cotton towns of Lancashire. Today this movement to the periphery is usually connected with the establishment of the capitalistic form of production in colonial and backward areas and, as such areas become independent states, these states use political methods to assert an economic independence based on local industry. 'Autarky' as a feature of the national state is a characteristic of modern times. In the Roman Empire the factors were somewhat simpler and more primitive.

Perhaps the most important reason for moving industry as near as possible to the new market was the weakness of ancient communications. Judged by preceding ages, Roman communications were highly developed; but in relation to the tasks the Empire set, they were still far too primitive. Land transport was slow and inefficient; for the ancient world never discovered the horse-collar, but employed a form of harness which half-strangled the beast and made oxen a better proposition for all heavy loads. A sea-voyage was always chancy, and overseas trade a hazardous business. Even by the time of Augustus the task of maintaining imperial communications was beginning to weight as an intolerable burden upon the inhabitants of the Empire. The cost of the Imperial Post, the upkeep of the roads, the housing of travelling officials—all these fell upon the provincial. And in spite of police and river flotillas, brigandage had not been wholly eliminated; the inns too were often poor and unevenly distributed. The dangers of a voyage in the early years of the Empire were very real. Perhaps St. Paul was unlucky in his adventures (including a shipwreck) on board the three vessels which were necessary to bring him from Palestine to Rome. Against his experience one can quote the case of Flavius Zeuxis of Hierapolis in Asia Minor, a merchant who made seventy-two voyages round the stormy Cape Malea to Italy and lived (his tombstone tells us) to die at home; and Paul himself had generally better fortune on his journeys. For all that, it remains true that the best transport system of the ancient world was inadequate to cope with a relatively high circulation of consumers' goods; and to make matters worse there is evidence that deterioration had set in from the time of Augustus onwards.

A second factor which impelled industry outwards towards its markets was the insecurity of ancient credit. Because of the risks entailed, it was always costly to raise capital for a trading venture; interest rates were high because the risk run was personal. There was no ancient equivalent of the joint-stock company with limited liability to ensure corporate responsibility for financial ventures; and banking itself remained primitive. The Empire saw no further development of the Ptolemaic system of a central bank with branch establishments; on the contrary, in Egypt there are signs of regression to a system of independent local banks.

Furthermore, the fact that ancient industry was based on slavery also influenced the movement of decentralization. For slavery as an institution was adversely affected by the Augustan peace. The steps the Emperors took to end war and piracy caused a drying-up of the main source of supply. The great days of the Delian slave market were gone for ever; and, though under the more humane conditions of the early Empire the number of home-reared slaves was quite considerable, they were not sufficient to fill the gap, so that increasingly the Roman world had to fall back on the small trickle from outside the frontiers. Besides this, the growth of humanitarian sentiment, already mentioned in chapter two, led to a widespread movement of slave-manumission. Cicero tells us that a diligent slave could save enough to buy his freedom in less than seven years; and many were led by unworthy motives to manumit their older slaves after the passing of the

Corn Bill of 58 B.C. so that as freedmen they might share in the free distributions at the expense of the State. Yesterday's slave was tomorrow's freedman; and his grandsons would be full Roman citizens. It has been calculated that during the thirty-two years preceding the civil war of 49 B.C. about half a million slaves were manumitted—an average of 16,000 a year. The movement was resisted by the government. We know of two laws dating from the Principate of Augustus—of 17 B.C. and 2 B.C. respectively— which attempted to limit manumission in various ways, including a sliding scale to be applied to testamentary liberation. The fact that this measure imposed an upper limit of 100 is some indication, however, of the size of the establishments still maintained by the nobles of the early Empire.

The weakening of the institution of slavery brought certain consequences in its train. In particular, the normal basis of ancient capitalistic activity was undermined; and the immediate results proved disastrous for the older centres of industry. Thus we observe a shifting of industry to more primitive lands where, as in Gaul, industry had available, if not new slaves, what was perhaps better, a free proletariat willing to turn its hands to manual labour. The discovery of a series of inscribed potsherds from la Graufesenque (Aveyron) has led to the suggestion that here a number of free craftsmen shared a common kiln, perhaps organized as a kind of producers' co-operative; and the discovery, in the most recent excavations on this site, of extensive pre-Roman potteries, suggests that this pattern of industry may go back to that period. This use of free labour, which we find also in Ptolemaic Egypt, is in marked contrast to the conditions existing in the potteries of Arretium in Italy, where, before A.D. 25, 123 out of 132 known workers were slaves. There is in fact no evidence for the employment of slaves in the potteries of Gaul and the Rhine valley; and inscriptions from Dijon refer to stone-workers and smiths as free dependents (*clientes*) of Ti. Flavius Vetus, evidently some local *seigneur*—an interesting sidelight on the break-up of the tribal system and the growth of social classes in Gaul. This shifting of industry contributed to the already mentioned urbanization of these backward parts; and here we may note that the new municipalities in such areas as Gaul and Spain inherited what the Italian municipalities had largely lost—a hinterland inhabited by peasants. Indeed it has been argued that by becoming each a little Rome in exploiting the dwellers in its own countryside the municipalities contributed on a long-term view to their own subsequent ruin.

Another important feature of industry based on slavery was that concentration brought no appreciable reduction of overhead expenses, as happens where power-machines are employed. Hence there was no incentive to develop the old centres rather than expand to new. Moreover, the simple nature of ancient equipment, the absence of complicated machinery, made it a comparatively easy business to move. Usually it would merely be a question of a few simple tools and the skill carried in a man's own fingers. On the other hand, the restricted internal market, which necessarily drove the merchant farther and farther afield, combined with the constant demands of a relatively prosperous army along the frontiers to reinforce the general centrifugal tendency of industry. Since the days of the Republic, the army had changed its economic role. Then, as the source of valuable plunder, it had paid its way over and over again. Now, as an instrument of Romanization and as a peaceful garrison force, its economic function was somewhat more complicated. In the occupation of a new province it would supervise the building of essential military works—forts, harbours, roads and bridges, frequently establishing its own brickworks and opening up quarries for the purpose. The next stage was the arrival of the Italian trader, with goods to serve the army and, incidentally, the local population. This was quickly followed by the growth of trading stations and market towns, such as Kempten in Allgäu; and very soon the final stage was reached with the development of production in what had originally been a colonial area. Industry had shifted outwards and the demand for Italian products diminished. In this typical development the army played a magnetic but passive role. Its other economic aspect however was as a liability, since it meant 250,000 to 300,000, and later as many as 400,000 idle mouths to feed—perhaps not an excessive figure out of a population of perhaps ninety millions, but none the less an item which, in view of the poor productivity of ancient labour, must certainly figure among the factors contributing to the decline of the Empire.

All these tendencies did not operate at once nor to the same extent; but over the years they resulted in a clear movement

Slave being flogged. A realistic painted figurine from Priene, originally suspended from a string.

Sale of a slave. The funeral *stele* of a freedman, Publilius Satur, from Cumae, depicts his original sale, when a slave; the dealer stands on the left in Greek dress, the purchaser in a toga on the right. The slave is naked.

Crane. Relief from the tomb of the Haterii family at Rome, now in the Lateran Museum; it shows a crane worked by a treadmill linked with a system of ropes and pulleys.

of industry outwards from the old centres of the Empire. One of the earliest developments was that trade became local and provincial instead of international; though, significantly, the drop in long-distance trade did not apply to luxury articles, which still travelled virtually any distance to meet the demands of the wealthy few. Over the whole Empire there was a gradual reversion to small-scale, hand-to-mouth craftsmanship, producing for the local market and for specific orders in the vicinity. The tendency is most easily traced in the history of the production of *terra sigillata*, the universal red-ware pottery of the early Empire. At the end of the Republic this ware was being manufactured at various centres in Italy, including Rome, Puteoli and in particular Arretium in Etruria. Under the early Empire Arretium has captured the market and its easily recognizable wares, produced in relatively large slave-manned potteries, are found all over the known world from North Gaul to Pondichéry. However the centre of production soon shifted northward, first to Modena, then to la Graufesenque and to several minor centres in southern Gaul, such as Banassac (Lozère) and Montans (Tarn). Shortly after Augustus's death pots from la Graufesenque appear on sites near the Rhine and Lippe, and for some thirty years its vast potteries had complete control of the market. In Domitian's reign examples penetrated as far north as Scotland. By this time however the industry was once more on the move. Between A.D. 75 and 110 the new centre was Lezoux, near Clermont-Ferrand, where the Allier offered a convenient means of transport. By this time the Italian industry was having difficulty in maintaining even the home market. Among the ruins of Pompeii an unopened crate of Gallic pottery offers a vivid illustration of the reality of this new competition. But the turn of Lezoux came next. Drawn irresistibly towards the military zone of the Rhine and the Danube, the industry shifted eastward to Alsace, the Rhine, the Moselle and the *limes*. From Hadrian's time onwards pots from Rheinzabern near Speyer are found throughout the whole Rheinland. Finally in A.D. 170 the Rheinzabern potters moved to Werstendorf in Bavaria. In Gaul, meanwhile, a secondary stage of decentralization had been reached with the appearance of a multiplicity of sites catering for a small local market with inferior wares. The same story could be repeated for other commodities, such as glassware, the makers of which migrated from Italy to Gaul in A.D. 50, to move on in stages from Arles to Namur, Trier, Worms and Cologne, or the lamps used and found in Africa, which were first Italian, then Carthaginian, and finally the product of purely local factories.

The progress made by the various provinces was naturally uneven; sometimes the first result of decentralization was to locate some important manufacture in particularly favourable surroundings; in which case the decentralized industry might for a time capture the international market. This, as we have seen, happened to the *terra sigillata* of la Graufesenque and Lezoux, which has been turned up in Italy, Spain, Africa, Britain and even in Syria and Egypt. Similarly Gallic wines were exported to the east from Narbonne and Arles until the middle of the third century of our era. But on the whole this was exceptional, and in the case of Gaul and Germany was perhaps due to geographical factors, especially the excellent water-transport system, and also the existence of cheap, free labour, conditions which were not reproduced in the eastern provinces with their more ancient town civilization.

Progress in such areas as Gaul and Roman Germany was balanced by the decay of Italy. During the second century A.D. this one-time kernel of the Empire lost increasingly its predominant position. As the western provinces gradually made themselves self-sufficient for all their main needs—grain, wine, oil, salt, glass, textiles, brassware and pottery—Italy became more and more parasitical upon the rest of the Empire. Northern Italy remained prosperous for a longer period, thanks to its links with the Danube provinces. But in the rest of the peninsula from the end of the first century A.D. onwards there appear signs of depopulation and a marked decline in the export of both agricultural and industrial products. As the trend towards decentralization developed, and as the Gallic wine-trade grew, the vineyards and olive fields of Italy shrank, making place increasingly for the cultivation of corn on large estates, farmed with serf-labour. Italy became an incubus, supported by invisible exports—taxes levied to maintain the civil service, and the vast proceeds from the emperor's private estates.

Simultaneously, at the opposite extreme, in the lands outside the frontiers, and especially to the north and north-east, among the Gauls, the Germans and the Scythians, the outward expansion of Roman trade and influence was inducing a ferment, which was to have far-reaching effects. Already the Gauls whom Caesar conquered (59–50 B.C.) and the Germans whom Tacitus described in his *Germania*, published in A.D. 98, had to some degree modified their earlier tribal organization; in both lands there were considerable differences of wealth, and rich counts had each their retinues of followers. But from the time of Augustus the natural development of these peoples was accelerated by the impact of Romanization. Increasingly they became involved in imperial trade-currents, buying and selling across the frontiers. Increasingly they enlisted in the Roman armies as mercenaries, and on retirement took their acquired habits back to their tribes like New Guinea natives returning home from Rabaul or Sydney. Romanized chieftains employed their new culture in the service of Rome, or like Arminius, against her. In short, the centrifugal economic movement did not and could not stop at the frontiers; but overflowing into the barbarian world beyond, it carried the virtues and vices of civilization like a strong wine to unaccustomed heads. It was the Romans themselves who taught the northern barbarians to look with interest and envy at the rich spoils of the Empire.

Meanwhile the process of decentralization and sub-division into smaller and smaller economic units continued. In itself, given the backward state of the productive forces, this movement was not regressive: indeed it prevented the wastage of much effort and wealth on the unnecessary movement of goods by means of an expensive transport system. Moreover, the drying-up of old trade routes was to some extent counter-balanced by the opening-up of new, in particular the great route along the valleys of the Rhine and Danube, which became more and more important from the time of Trajan (A.D. 98–117) and was later consolidated by the establishment of the northern capitals at Trier, Milan, Sirmium (Mitrovitza), Serdica and Constantinople. But in some degree this drift away from the centre to the periphery was a movement making for disintegration; and the move northward beyond the Alps helped to shift the balance of an empire which had grown up around the Mediterranean—*mare nostrum*. Politically the same movement was reflected in the division of the empire, first of all in the elaborate four-fold administration of Diocletian and his three colleagues (A.D. 286), later, after Constantine had transferred the capital to Byzantium (A.D. 330), in the permanent division into an eastern and western Empire, which embodied the two persistent and divergent traditions of the Latin West and the Greek East. Out of this division came the Greek renaissance in the Byzantine State and the foundations of mediaeval Europe in the West.

Fundamental too for mediaeval Europe was one particular aspect of this general movement of decentralization—the gradual transfer of industry from the cities to the villages and large country estates. In this way the essentially agrarian character of ancient civilization began to re-assert itself over the urban elements which had produced its highest and most typical developments; the depressed countryside took its revenge for the long centuries during which its needs were subordinated to those of the smart men of the towns. In Italy, as we saw, vineyards and olive gardens now began to make way for large corn-growing estates: in short, intensive cultivation gave way to a less efficient and less specialized system. Since the early days of the Republic there had been a tendency for large farms to absorb small, and particularly in the second century B.C. the growth of *latifundia* in Tuscany, parts of Latium and Campania, and the south of Italy, had become a serious threat to the prosperity of Italy. As we saw (above, pp. 32–3), this movement had to some extent been mitigated by the granting of small allotments to city dwellers and retired veterans under the legislation of the Gracchi, Sulla and Caesar; but there were still note-worthy, if exceptional, examples of estates on a tremendous scale. Thus Caesar records[1] how in 49 B.C. Domitius Ahenobarbus, one of Pompey's generals in the civil war, attempted to ensure his soldiers' allegiance in a tight corner by promising each man between two and three acres out of his own private estates. If this applied only to his own army of 4,000 out of the 15,000 men under his command, it implies very considerable possessions. Later, in Nero's reign, Pliny tells us,[2] six men owned half the province of Africa; and increasingly under the Empire the large estate becomes the typical unit of land ownership. Moreover, it began to develop in a way which ultimately transformed its character and with it the whole system of classical economy.

1. Caesar, *Bell. civ.* i, 17.   2. *Nat. hist.* xviii, 35.

In the first place, the large country estate had always been the scene of a certain amount of industry. Specially trained slaves had done the necessary farm jobs, tanning, weaving, wagon-making, fulling and work in the carpenter's or blacksmith's shop. By A.D. 50 Pliny assumes the presence of such craftsmen to be a normal feature of any estate; and by the time of Vespasian (A.D. 69–79) the Emperor's own estates, organized on the pattern of the royal domains of the Hellenistic period, were setting the fashion in the provinces by becoming increasingly an agglomeration of crafts-men of every kind, as well as agricultural labourers—in fine, a self-contained community of a type common to the old Bronze Age civilizations, and later, as the manor, to mediaeval Christendom. Notable examples of such villas have been unearthed in Gaul. The magnificent establishment of Anthée near Namur consisted of a central house surrounded by some twenty separate buildings, at least half of which seem to have been used for industrial purposes —as foundries and breweries and for the production of bronze and enamelled articles, pottery, harness and leather work. Similarly a villa found at Chiragan near Toulouse was the centre of a cluster of about eighty smaller buildings, of which many had been used for industry. Whether this industry was directed primarily to home needs or the market cannot always be determined. But as the self-contained estate becomes in-creasingly a feature of the countryside of Africa, S. Russia, Italy, Asia Minor, Babylonia, Palestine and Syria, it appears to aim at profit as well as the satisfying of home requirements. With the general crisis of the third century, which hit the towns hardest, it was on such estates that economic life remained most vigorous.

The gradual drying-up of the sources of slave-labour compelled the landowner to seek some other supply. Increasingly he turned to the *coloni*, not sturdy independent peasants of the old Italian type, but tenant-farmers, successors of the obsolescent slave class to the doubtful privilege of being the bottom dog in the country-side. These *coloni* were usually too poor to pay rent for their land or to buy their own implements and seed; these they obtained from the landlord and, as 'share-croppers', repaid him in kind and, in some provinces such as Africa, by services on his private land. Subsistence agriculture along these lines required neither traditional skill nor experience: it offered the 'new rich', who arose out of the various crises of the state, an opportunity to increase their fortunes in a safe and easy fashion.

The factor of inadequate transport, already considered above, also helped the growth of these self-sufficient industrial estates. By making everything on the spot, the late Roman precursor of the feudal baron would eliminate the most costly item in his bill of expenses. It is not surprising that this sort of 'nuclear' economy tended to attach itself to any kind of large unit engaged in primary production. Not only large industrial estates, but also mining camps, fisheries and hunting parks appear as the nuclei around which handicrafts and industries agglomerated themselves. Thus as early as the first century, the mining village at Vipasca (Aljustrel in what is now southern Portugal) contained barbers, fullers, shoemakers and other craftsmen, whose activities (since this was an imperially owned estate) were carefully controlled by legal enactment. Sometimes these primary units were temple property, not only recalling the similar institutions of Babylon or Hellenistic Asia Minor, but also foreshadowing clearly the mediaeval monastery. Similarly, the new, depressed class of *coloni* were the forerunners of the later serfs.

From the time of Augustus onwards this form of 'domain' economy was encroaching gradually upon the old capitalist system, based on slave-labour and the free market; and it was soon followed by a catastrophic drop in every branch of agricultural technique. It is significant that after the first century A.D. agricultural literature ceased to exist as a creative force, and in its place we find the mechanical transcribing of ancient works. Yet, notwithstanding this decline in the efficiency of agricultural technique, the land continued to exercise a magnetic attraction as conditions in the towns deteriorated. In the next chapter we shall analyse how and why the state found itself obliged to make ever greater financial demands upon the bourgeoisie. From this pressure, the 'nuclear' estate, worked by the methods of subsistence economy, under the protection of some powerful landlord, offered its owner a safe retreat.

This flight of industry from the towns to the manorial estates itself contributed to the general economic breakdown by reducing the effective areas open to trade. Each estate, in proportion as it became self-sufficing, meant so many more individuals subtracted from the classical economic system, so many less potential consumers for those commodities which still circulated on the old markets. So the large domain played its part in restricting trade and speeding up the general process of decentralization.

By now it must be apparent that Gibbon's picture of Rome under the Antonines needs considerable qualification. For we have traced several factors of decline rooted in the structure of Roman society, which were already beginning to operate from the time of Augustus (27 B.C.–A.D. 14), and were certainly in full swing during the period which Gibbon praised for its unique felicity. We have seen how the low level of technique in Graeco-Roman civilization had led to the development of slavery as a means of purchasing the leisure necessary for comfort and culture; and how this institution operated on both slave and master to rule out the possibility of releasing new productive forces on a scale adequate to change the material conditions of society. We have seen the restricted internal market, which followed inevitably from a social structure of this kind, bringing its own nemesis in the shape of an outward drive to seek fresh markets away from the old centres of civilization. We have seen how the backwardness of credit institutions and of communications, and the drying-up of the slave-supply itself, served to reinforce this decentralizing movement, which was eventually to find its political counterpart in the division and (in the West) in the ultimate disintegration of the Empire. And finally we have noted the growth of the large estate, the symbol of the decline of urban civilization, and both a result of the general decay and a factor in hastening it. We must analyse next the reaction of the imperial State to these trends, and trace the further process of disintegration and decay.

NOTES FOR FURTHER READING

On the question of the level of ancient technique in general see two popular works by V. Gordon Childe, *Man Makes Himself*, London, Thinker's Library, 1941, and *What Happened in History*, Harmondsworth, Pelican Books, 1942; also *Science in Antiquity*, London, Home University Library, 1936, and *Greek Science: its Meaning for Us.* Vol. I *Thales to Aristotle;* Vol. II *Theophrastus to Galen*, Harmondsworth, Pelican Books, 1944 and 1949 by B. Farrington. Two books by the same author, *Science and Politics in the Ancient World*, London, 1939, and *Head and Hand in Ancient Greece*, London, Thinker's Library, 1947, discuss the effects of the social cleavage on ancient thought. The inventions of the classical world are related to later discoveries and the legacy both of the barbarians and of the far east in an article by L. White, *Speculum*, xv, 1940, pp. 141–59, 'Technology and invention in the Middle Ages'; this discusses the important works of Lefebvre des Noëttes, *L'Attelage et le cheval de selle à travers les âges*, Paris, 1931 (on harness) and *De la marine antique à la marine moderne: la révolution du gouvernail*, Paris, 1936, and also affords an invaluable bibliography on other similar topics. See further the books mentioned in the notes to Chapter II, and Oertel's chapter in *Cambridge Ancient History*, Vol. XII (1939), pp. 232–81, 'The economic life of the Empire'; also the present writer's chapter on the trade and industry of the later empire in *Cambridge Economic History of Europe*, Vol. II (1942), pp. 33–85, with bibliography pp. 523–8 (new edition in preparation). On slavery see R. H. Barrow, *Slavery in the Roman Empire*, London, 1928: also two articles by M. I. Finley, *Historia*, 1959, pp. 145–64, and by A. H. M. Jones, *Eng. Historical Review*, 1950, pp. 185–99, both of which are reprinted in *Slavery in Classical Antiquity* (Cambridge, Heffer, 1960), a useful selection of reprinted articles from various sources, edited by M. I. Finley.

4

SHRINKAGE AND CRISIS

TO isolate the moment when a society ceases to progress and begins to decay is never easy. The factors involved are so numerous, and concern phenomena at such diverse stages of development, that vigorous expansion in one sphere may well coincide with already advanced decay in another. But, if there is such a moment in the history of the Roman Empire, it falls in the year A.D. 117, when Hadrian succeeded Trajan to the Principate.

Under Trajan the Empire achieved its farthest territorial extension; now Dacia beyond the Danube, Armenia and Mesopotamia beyond the Euphrates, were incorporated in the Empire. Trajan's primary objects were strategic; his annexation of Dacia was the reply to interference from its king, Decebalus, who had forced Domitian to pay *danegeld*, while in his eastern policy he was seeking a radical solution to the secular conflict with Parthia. At the same time this military policy coincided with the general economic movement outwards. For the classical area of trade was greater than the Empire. From the time of Claudius it is possible to identify several large trading areas, not isolated from one another, but including within their frontiers (which might embrace several administrative provinces) the bulk of their trade. Thus Spain, Germany and Britain were grouped around Gaul. In Africa the provinces from Mauretania to Cyrenaica went together. A third grouping, which increasingly lost economic strength, consisted of Italy, together with the islands of Sicily, Corsica and Sardinia. Anchored to this block through the trade of Aquileia was the Danube group from Rhaetia in the west to Dacia (and South Russia) in the east. Similarly Greece, Macedon, Thrace, Asia Minor and Armenia were bound together by ancient traditions and Hellenic culture as well as commerce; and a further block embraced Syria, Babylon and Iran, an area half Roman and half Parthian in its political alignment. Sooner or later it was likely that an attempt would be made to unite as much as possible of this eastern block within the political frontiers on the one side or the other; and it was this task that Trajan accomplished.

In doing so, however, he stretched the financial and military resources of the Empire to the breaking-point; and even before Hadrian succeeded, there is evidence for a reversal of policy. It now appears that the more southerly of Trajan's conquests—if indeed they were ever firmly in Roman hands—the district of Parapotamia between the lower reaches of the Tigris and the Euphrates, and the city of Dura, had already been handed back to the new king of Parthia before Trajan's death. Hadrian continued this revised policy, relinquishing the rest of the territory beyond the Euphrates; and by a policy of peaceful consolidation he brought the Empire the relief which is reflected in the prosperity of the *pax Hadriani*. As a second Augustus, Hadrian toured the Empire, supervising its effective frontier dispositions and organising its provinces with wholly admirable solicitude. Yet the limits which were thus set to its expansion were an ominous sign that the peak of its creative energy had been reached.

The growth of the Empire had been part of a process of political unification, corresponding to the economic unification of the ancient world; from that point of view Julius Caesar and Augustus were, as we saw, the direct successors of Alexander the Great. It has been argued that, had he lived, Caesar meant to extend the frontiers yet further, and carry out Trajan's programme a century and a half before his time. Be that as it may, what is quite clear is that by the time of Trajan further expansion had become a task to which the resources of the Empire were no longer equal. In fact, Hadrian and his successors found themselves in a dilemma. The movement of economic decentralization towards the periphery of the Empire furnished incentive to extend the frontiers yet wider, and to annex for Rome those areas which already enjoyed close commercial links with the Empire. In this way it might have been possible to open up yet further fields of foreign trade to compensate for that absence of a deep internal market which followed inevitably from the structure of ancient society. But without some increase in general productivity such an expansion could only have resulted in a further decentralization, leaving the inner parts of the Empire to suffer the fate of Italy; and the cost of administration and the manning of an extended frontier must have accentuated a pressure on the citizens of the Empire which had already begun to grow acute. In fact, the tendencies already examined above had, in the century and a half which divided Julius Caesar from Trajan, put any such development beyond the range of practical politics.

Over the whole period from the first century to the time of Marcus Aurelius (A.D. 161–80) there are clear indications of a fall in the population; a comparison of figures taken from Egypt and Palestine with the sums paid in connection with the manumission of slaves at Delphi during the same period shows a general fall of prices alongside a rise in wages—phenomena which together confirm the general picture given in the literary sources of a universal decline in the population of the Empire. Moreover, as in Greece, during the crisis of the second century B.C., the bourgeoisie in particular were refusing to rear families. That this trend set in early is clear from the legislation which Augustus directed against it, legislation which would not have been constantly reaffirmed and have remained in force for three centuries, had the authorities not felt it to be both urgent and at least partially effective. Equally, for reasons we must shortly consider, the richer classes in the towns declined more and more to accept their military responsibilities for the defence of the Empire; even the ordinary offices of administration which their ancestors had filled with pride now seemed a financial burden which they were loath to shoulder. In short, the resources and the manpower of the Empire were no longer adequate to the demands made upon them, still less to the pursuance of Trajan's policy of expansion, which was from many points of view the logical development of the Empire.

The contraction of the population and the shrinkage of resources were not, unfortunately, accompanied by a decline in the cost of imperial administration. An empire stretching from Northumberland to the Euphrates, from the Carpathians to the Sahara, could not reduce its expenses below a certain minimum. Governors had to be sent out, taxes collected, frontiers garrisoned; the Empire had to be policed, its waters swept clear of pirates, roads kept in order, the imperial post maintained. Of the vast network of cities which were the guardians of ancient culture, each had its own local problems of municipal administration, its council of *decuriones*, with a certain prestige to maintain in the provision of appropriate buildings, festivals and benefactions; and the upholding of the

Roman standard of culture demanded throughout this wide area an adequate supply of the amenities of civilized life—baths, gymnasia, theatres, amphitheatres, wrestling-schools, aqueducts, town halls, ceremonial arches, elaborate tombs, triumphal columns, market-places, colonnades and temples—all of them considered essential to the full life of a Roman citizen. Life in the towns was always extravagant. It has been pointed out that the ancient world not only failed to develop the productivity of labour, but also failed to produce the puritanism which has so often gone side by side with that development. The rich town-dweller squandered his riches or invested them in land: in neither case did he add to the wealth of the community. In addition the costs of the court with its luxuries, and its grants of 'bread and circuses' to the pampered metropolis, were by no means a negligible item of the imperial budget; and when, in the third and fourth centuries, the administration was subdivided, and as many as four courts had to be maintained simultaneously, the burden became all but insupportable.

The Empire possessed no larger resources to meet this heavy bill in a time of contraction. Indeed, private indebtedness was so widespread as to be a damper on economic enterprise, and in A.D. 118 Hadrian agreed to wipe off a bad debt to the treasury of 900 million sesterces, and subsequently remitted many sums outstanding for rent. But when the citizens of the Empire could not pay, remission of debts was clearly no permanent solution. The problem was quite simply to make sixpence do the work of a shilling; and the whole question of finance became cardinal from the second century onwards. Sooner or later tax-payers must be compelled to find what the State demanded: which in turn implied that the State must be strengthened, since it must, in its new role of extortioner, become increasingly the enemy of the ordinary man. Under the early Principate the policy had been to encourage the towns of Italy and the Empire to model themselves on Rome, and to run their own affairs. In the east the Greek system of having a primary assembly, a council elected for a short period, and annual magistrates, had been gradually abolished in favour of the Roman type of municipal organization, which, as we saw (above, p. 22), was able, through its controlled assembly and council elected for life, to restrict the activities of the annual magistrates and ensure that the real power was in the hands of the wealthy. This implied a kind of partnership between the government at Rome and the rich families in the municipalities. But with the growth of the bureaucracy, and of those features of administration which we regard today as the mark of the 'police-state', this alliance broke down. It is a melancholy reflection that the emperors were led to extract by force from their subjects the revenues that in the hardier days of the republic had been provided by the plunder of foreign war; and that the counterpart of the *pax Romana* was legalized extortion.

Both Trajan and Hadrian are reckoned among the 'five good emperors'. Personally their characters left little ground for criticism; they had the good of the Empire at heart and they laboured unceasingly on its behalf. To Pausanias, who lived under his two successors, Hadrian was the ruler 'who gave the utmost to all for the happiness of the world'. Yet it is under precisely these two emperors that the first ugly signs of bureaucratic tyranny appear. If we neglect an uncertain example dating from A.D. 92, the first use of special commissioners to supervise the internal affairs of the cities occurs under Trajan. These *curatores* concerned themselves particularly with the free cities and reported directly to the emperor. From the time of Hadrian their numbers increase, and they tend more and more to be appointed to supervise individual cities. By the early third century, they have become a normal imperial office, which eventually goes to a local man and degenerates into one more magistracy. But by this time new forms of control and coercion had been devised. Under Trajan too we find the growth of a system of obligatory state leases, and the compulsory recruitment of local officials for the lower and middle grades of the civil service.

It is under Hadrian, however, that a more odious phenomenon appears—the secret police and informers, who evolved out of the commissariat officials known as *frumentarii*. As pressure upon the cities increased, so naturally did the resistance of their populations, and this inevitably led to the appointment of more civil servants and spies. The time had not yet come when Lactantius would complain bitterly that there were more people living off the taxes than paying them; but the first steps had been taken, and from the time of Hadrian onwards this secret police force functioned uninterruptedly till its modification by Diocletian. The fact that it was an emperor so enlightened as Hadrian who introduced it suggests some degree of inevitability in its development. At the same time the government tried to maintain the support of the local aristocracies; there is some evidence, especially from the provinces of Asia Minor, that under the façade of the first and second century prosperity, there was serious popular discontent and sharpened contrasts. We read of class conflicts at Smyrna, Rhodes and Sardis, of riots and arson in Prusa; and it has been plausibly suggested that the imperial government, unable to make radical concessions to the populace, which would have preferred cheaper food and circuses to elaborate building programmes, deliberately attempted to consolidate the caste of the local aristocracy, as a useful ally, by grants of senatorial rank. But this tended to separate them from the fortunes of their cities, and thus rendered the burden all the greater on those who remained responsible for the local administration and taxes.

Already therefore in the second century, beneath the rosy hues of the Antonine regime, weaknesses and stresses were developing. In the third century the crisis became open and catastrophic. The faint rumblings along the north-east frontiers, which by the late second century A.D. had swelled sufficiently loud to draw the philosophic Marcus Aurelius from the study to the camp, now burst out into the full disaster of large-scale barbarian invasion. In this emergency all turned on the army. But for several reasons the army was no longer reliable. The theory of an elected emperor was a constant incitement to ambitious army leaders, and these were frequently able to exploit the devotion of troops to whom the State as an object of allegiance was meaningless. This was all the easier because the armies were themselves recruited more and more from among the barbarians. Since the early Empire we find a constant (and not unsuccessful) policy of settling the frontier peoples on Roman soil; thus Nero's governor of Moesia, Ti. Plautius Silvanus Aelianus, claimed credit for having transported 100,000 men from across the Danube. Such men as these furnished the troops which the Empire could no longer afford to raise from among the reliable sectors of the population in the more advanced provinces; and in fighting against barbarians their technique was frequently better than that hallowed by Roman tradition. But technique was no adequate substitute for loyalty and reliability, and a barbarized army ready to revolt at the bidding of an ambitious general was no longer the force to garrison the Empire.

The machinery of government broke down; civil war gave rise to chaos; emperors were duplicated; and invasions followed each other with dismal regularity. The attacks of the Marcomanni and Quadi in A.D. 166 were eventually put down after great efforts, but the revolt of Avidius Cassius in the east prevented a final settlement. In the third century the main threat came from the Goths, who had acquired the military arts of the nomads of the steppes during their sojourn near the Black Sea. But in addition there was trouble in other provinces. Already in A.D. 173 the Moors had pillaged Spain; and in the east a new foe arose in Sassanid Persia. By the middle of the third century the emperor Gallienus was reduced to taking a daughter of the king of the Marcommani as wife, and awarding consular insignia to a chieftain of the fierce Heruli, who in A.D. 267 ravaged Greece and the Balkans. The Alamanni he defeated at Milan in A.D. 258, but had to relinquish control of Rhaetia and what is now Baden.

About the same time the Franks penetrated Gaul, took upwards of sixty cities and made this province a base for raids along the Spanish seaboard. Further east the Goths passed through Moesia and Thrace to sack many of the ancient cities of Asia Minor, including Calchedon, Nicomedia, Nicaea and Prusa. Despite the efforts of the emperors, the imperial defences proved insufficient; and far too many of the ruling class failed to realize the significance of what they were witnessing. A late third century rhetorician comments on the passing of captured barbarians through the towns, an object of ridicule to citizens who had but yesterday shuddered at their approach, and now foresaw their transformation into harmless peasants, haggling in the market and selling their produce, which should raise the standard of life for themselves, the townsfolk. Such minds as these had not begun to understand what was happening to Roman civilization.

To many the army itself seemed a greater scourge than the enemy. From what is now Aga Bey Köy in Anatolia came the appeal of imperial tenants to some third century emperor against the threats from the military police (*colletiones*):

To tell your divinity the truth, unless your heavenly right hand exert some justice for these wrongs and bring aid for the future, those of us who are left, unable to endure the greed of the *colletiones*, must desert our ancestral homes and family tombs and move to private property to preserve ourselves; for wrongdoers are more inclined to spare the dwellers there than they are your farmers.

Similar appeals went up to Gordian III in A.D. 238 from the peasants of Scaptopara in Thrace; and from Libanius in the fourth century we hear of farmers turned brigand in sheer desperation. Town and village alike suffered under this scourge, and from various parts of the Empire came these pathetic appeals to the Emperor who, it was felt, could still save his people if he only knew.

It was the lower classes who bore the full weight of the burden. For a time the upper class lived on its capital and managed to pass on the intolerable hardships to the classes it was itself exploiting; until the masses, provoked beyond endurance by heavy taxes, regimentation and falling wages, fell back upon strikes, and finally upon insurrection or appeals to the barbarians themselves. In the fourth century writers such as Ammianus and Themistius testify to the popular support which was often afforded to the invaders; and elsewhere we read that they were saved from starvation by the aid of the peasants who directed them to the Roman food stores. In Gaul, and especially in the west, a peasant *jacquerie* waged a series of wars against the imperial government, which lasted from about A.D. 284 until the middle of the fifth century. Under the name of *Bagaudae* (probably a Celtic word meaning 'those in revolt') they succeeded in occupying whole areas in the west and administering justice 'under the greenwood tree'. Paulinus of Pella describes them as 'a servile faction with an intermixture of freeborn youths, raving mad, and armed for the especial murder of the nobility'; but Salvian of Marseilles regards their successes in the fifth century as being, like those of the barbarians, the retribution of God for the wickedness of the Romans; and like Paulinus he admits that even men of substance and liberal education have joined them. The Gallic landowners recognized the threat from this movement and in A.D. 437 they did not hesitate to employ the barbarous Huns under their leader Litorius to put down these peasants in revolt, a defeat from which the movement however quickly recovered. About the same period we hear of activity of the Bagaudae in Spain as well. In Egypt too the documents reveal appalling conditions, villages depopulated, peasants everywhere deserting their homes to avoid unbearable responsibilities. A German scholar has estimated that between the time of Augustus and A.D. 300 the total population of the Empire fell by approximately a third, from seventy to fifty millions.

In these terrible times the Emperors did not despair of the State. But the remedy was frequently more appalling than the evil it was designed to cure. To invasion and chaos, shrinking towns and peasants in flight or revolt, they had one answer—to tighten the bureaucracy and strengthen the instruments of the State, the army, the tax-collector and the secret police. In particular, from the time of Septimius Severus (A.D. 193–211), the army and the civil service were given special privileges, the far-reaching effects of which can scarcely be over-estimated. To understand these, it is necessary to turn to the monetary policy of the government. Augustus had stabilized the relationship between the gold *aureus*, minted from Julius Caesar's time onwards, and the older silver *denarius*, at 25:1, which represented a gold:silver ratio of about 12:1. Pliny tells us[1] that Nero reduced the *aureus* from $\frac{1}{40}$ to $\frac{1}{45}$, and the *denarius* from $\frac{1}{84}$ to $\frac{1}{96}$ of a pound, a statement confirmed by weighing specimens. There may also have been some reduction in the silver content of the *denarius*. Subsequently Trajan and the second century emperors reduced this silver content to 75 per cent. The cause of these adjustments is debated. But the reduction in the size of both silver and gold coins by Nero looks like a concession to strained finances; and M. Aurelius was undoubtedly trying to replenish an impoverished treasury. A little later Septimius Severus reduced the silver content of the *denarius* to 50 per cent, with the result that the coin began to be refused outright in Germany, where second-century hoards reveal an increased amount of gold. This debasement of the currency was tantamount to an inflation of silver in terms of gold. There was a sudden rise in prices, and when the legions protested against payment in bad money, they were successful in securing an increase in pay. But apparently they secured more than that. For it is under Septimius Severus that we must look for

1. *Nat. hist.* xxxiii, 47.

the beginnings of the system under which for their basic needs the army and civil service were paid not in cash, but in kind. Through a special order, which came to be of more and more frequent occurrence, instructions were conveyed to the province through which the route of the legions lay for the furnishing of their supplies, and this impost was known as *annona militaris*. Evidence of this tax, which represents the first regular attempt to set up a permanent organization to pay for the army, appears in Egypt at the end of the second century, and it is regularly collected throughout the third. An annual edict defined its terms for the coming year.

This system was of some advantage to the army and bureaucracy during the inflations of the third century, for it enabled them to avoid the effects of being paid in bad money—though some money payments continued in addition at least until the time of Diocletian (A.D. 284–305). However, by the end of the century their real standard of living had greatly declined, since they now received virtually nothing beyond their rations, uniform and arms. Moreover, the effects of the *annona* in other departments of economic life were far-reaching and unforeseen. In the first place the payment of taxes in kind inevitably raised problems of transport and compelled the setting up of public storehouses (*mansiones*) along the main highways of the Empire. State employees and the armed forces received their wages in the form of vouchers, which served as drafts on specified public stores in the neighbourhood. The recipient went to the appropriate *mansio* to draw his allowance of corn, wine or oil. Clearly the setting up of such a fiscal system involved a tremendous machinery of supply; and to meet this need the third and early fourth century emperors, and especially the most forceful of them, Septimius Severus (A.D. 193–211), Aurelian (A.D. 270–5), Diocletian (A.D. 284–305) and Constantine (A.D. 306–37), turned to an institution which had once held a high place among the amenities of a free society, but was now ingeniously transformed to provide the iron shackles of an authoritarian state.

NOTES FOR FURTHER READING

See the books already mentioned after chapters II and III. On the crisis of the third century after Christ see H. M. D. Parker, *A History of the Roman World, A.D.138–337*, London, 1935, and the relevant chapters in *Cambridge Ancient History*, Vol. XII. On the *annona militaris* see D. van Berchem, *Mém. de la soc. nat. des antiqu. de France*, LXXX, 1937, pp. 117–202; 'L'Annone militaire', and a survey of the imperial age by A. Passerini, *Linee di storia romana in età imperiale*, Milan, 1949, pp. 210 ff. All aspects of the organization of the later empire are dealt with in a masterly work by A. H. M. Jones, *The Later Roman Empire: a Social, Economic and Administrative Survey*, Oxford, 1964, 4 vols.; the specific problem of its decline is discussed in Vol. 2, pp. 1025–68.

5

THE AUTHORITARIAN STATE

THROUGHOUT the Hellenistic world, and more especially in Ptolemaic Egypt, we find countless associations or guilds of people engaged in similar work; their functions were partly religious and partly those of the modern friendly society or burial club, and to some extent they protected the professional interests of their members, without ever approaching the status of the modern trade union. As early as 200 B.C. we hear of a *collegium* (or guild) in Sardinia, of cooks from Falerii in Italy; but under the Republic such *collegia* were looked on with disfavour as potential sources of disorder, and they had been repeatedly banned. In 7 B.C. Augustus legalized them, provided that they were useful to the State. It is in connection with the guild of shippers, the *navicularii*, that the new policy is most apparent. These shippers were responsible for transporting to Rome the grain on which the capital subsisted, and therefore they were the object of special imperial solicitude. Under Claudius (A.D. 41–54) the exchequer offered concessions to such shippers and merchants (*negotiatores*) as undertook to build a ship of a little over thirty tons and employ it in the government service for six years. These concessions were confirmed by later emperors; but with the decline in the trade in goods for mass consumption which became apparent during the first century after Christ, it became customary for men engaged in water transport to combine this with some other occupation. Consequently under Hadrian (A.D. 117–38) the State began to insist that to be eligible for these concessions a shipper or merchant must employ the bulk of his capital on state duties.

As such arrangements assumed increasingly greater importance, the corporate bodies, or *collegia*, of the *navicularii* and *negotiatores* began to take the place of the individual traders in the contracts; and in the course of the third century it became clear that the further organization of these guilds was essential to the running of the new fiscal system. Already under Antoninus Pius (A.D. 138–61) the *navicularii* of Arles (who as a *collegium* enjoyed a private office in Beirut) are honouring their 'excellent and upright patron', the local procurator of the corn supply. M. Aurelius (A.D. 161–80) lays it down that no-one shall belong to more than one guild. But it is under Septimius Severus (A.D. 193–211) that a clear picture of the pattern emerges. It is now specifically stated that concessions can be claimed only by guildsmen who give their personal services, not by guildsmen promiscuously—a clear indication of the role the guilds had come to play in negotiations with the government. At the same time there appear *collegia* of smiths (who may have had duties as a fire-brigade even under the late Republic), oil merchants, bakers, corn-measurers and swine-merchants, all operating at Rome, except for the *navicularii*, who formed a kind of Merchant Navy active all over the Empire. In A.D. 200 the five *collegia* of Arles shippers went on strike to exact higher rates from the government.

Throughout the third century the role of the guilds continued to develop, and their freedom and status to decline. What were originally honourable and independent associations became instruments of state domination. Both the details and the causes of this development are partly obscured by the paucity of the third century sources. No doubt special factors operated in the various branches of production and distribution. But there seems good reason to regard the institution of the *annona*, the payment of the armed forces and civil service in kind, as one of the main contributory reasons. Another, no doubt, was the fact that private enterprise, left to itself, was proving unequal to the task of feeding the civilian population, and the State felt itself obliged to step in. What can be said with certainty is that by the end of the third century of our era the *collegia* have been transformed into controlled organizations, the members of which are tied to their occupation and pass on their obligations to their heirs. They were still treated with honour; they might still own possessions, and they had, as before, their patrons and religious observances; their members were exempt from many taxes and their retired presidents frequently received honorific titles. But increasingly the *collegia* became the instrument by which men's freedom of action was limited. More and more their activities were harnessed to the service of the State. Their members were forbidden to change their occupations and in some trades, like that of baker, they must choose their wives from the families of their fellow-guildsmen.

As an example let us take the case of the shippers. In the fourth century any *navicularius* owning a ship of something over thirty tons was compelled to put it at the disposal of the government, and in turn received certain tax reliefs, which after A.D. 326 amounted to a complete immunity from fiscal charges. In A.D. 380 he was given the status of *eques*, or knight. On the other hand, his duties were heavy. While he was engaged in transporting state cargoes, he was compensated at a figure defined in a legal enactment of A.D. 334 as 4 per cent of the value of a corn cargo in kind plus a thousandth of its value in gold—in order that he might carry out these duties 'with enthusiasm and scarcely any loss to himself'. But by the early fifth century the figure had fallen to 1 per cent of the cargo. Moreover, the shipper was hedged about with a nightmarish list of regulations, forbidding him to speculate with his cargo, linger *en route*, sabotage his ship, or attempt illicit trading under pain of death.

This special attention to the shippers clearly sprang from the importance of provisioning Rome, where 3,600,000 bushels of corn were needed each year to meet the claims of the public service and those entitled to free rations; and, as we saw (above, p. 30), if one includes the cheap corn which was provided for the rest of the population of the capital, the total consumption cannot have been much below 17,000,000 bushels. When at some date before Aurelian (A.D. 270–5), the distribution of bread was substituted for that of corn, the guilds of bakers, which had been officially recognized under Trajan, assumed new importance; and by the fourth century they too are completely integrated in the state service. Their property was linked with their occupation, which was inherited along with it. If a man became heir to the estates of both a shipper and a baker he was liable for both sets of duties; and anyone who married a baker's daughter must himself adopt her father's trade.

Corn was not, however, the only concern of the government. Free distribution of olive oil, which had taken place on various occasions since the later Republic, became regular from the time of Septimius Severus, and two guilds of oil merchants dealt with Spain and Africa respectively. Similarly, towards the end of the third century, with the regular distribution of a pork ration at Rome, the swine merchants acquired official duties, which involved collecting the animals from those who paid these as part of their tax in kind, driving them to Rome, and there having them slaughtered, so that they might be distributed as meat.

This growth in the principle of state distributions, and the institution of the military *annona* in connection with the army, had as their corollary a substantial development in the State transport system to convey the fiscal products to their various destinations. Here again the emperors used the familiar method of compulsory requisitioning. For some purposes humble muleteers were employed, for other the so-called *cursus publicus*, the imperial post, was adapted—a convenient improvisation, since it seems likely that the warehouses in which the goods were stored were set up in conjunction with posting stations along the main highways. These stations were under the control of members of those families in the nearby town, who were responsible for the filling of the local councils, and were now pressed into this additional service. The stables for the mules and oxen were built by *corvées* of forced labour, and the animals themselves were acquired and, when necessary, replaced by requisitioning. On the other hand the regular low-grade staff—grooms, muleteers and veterinary surgeons—were state employees.

Gradually a system had grown up under which the State distributed basic rations of bread, wine, oil and pork either free or very cheaply, and in return exacted compulsory services from the guildsmen. By the fourth century A.D. the picture revealed by the legal codes is one of complete state control over the individual. Not only a few selected professions, but all trades and occupations are now organized in hereditary *collegia*. We hear, for example, of guilds of inn-keepers, fishmongers, potters and silversmiths. Nor did this apply merely to Rome. Every town of any size had its own *collegia*, operating under the control of the local town council, the members of which were responsible to Rome for the implementation of their instructions. Examples are known from Aquileia, Lyons, Arles, Trier, Constantinople and Cyzicus, to mention but a few cities from which records have come down. The system is not one of full nationalization, but rather a mixed form of controlled private enterprise. The guildsman continues to own his industrial and commercial property. But instead of entering into a free contract for a specified period, he is compulsorily bound to work for the State by virtue of his ownership. In return he receives compensation for the loss of income; but this 'consolation', or *solacium*, as it was officially termed, increasingly takes the form of a payment in kind. Perhaps the last stage in the development is reached when enrolment in one or other of the *collegia* appears as an official penalty imposed on a convicted criminal who has hitherto avoided 'incorporation'.

The application of compulsion to the guildsmen from the third century onwards can be paralleled in the sphere of municipal government. Throughout the towns of the Empire the ruling groups were in the main landowners; and they found themselves hard hit by the requirements of the *annona militaris* which, as it was designed to meet an invariable demand, was a fixed amount, and not proportionate to the yield of the harvest. This burden, together with a crisis in the financial system which, as we shall see, broke down in a catastrophic inflation, served to exhaust the resources of many of the richer town families. An Egyptian papyrus of A.D. 250 tells of a certain Aurelius Hermophilus of Hermopolis who, after holding the municipal office of *kosmetes* at great personal expense, is now trying to obtain his son's release from a similar 'honour' by offering the authorities the whole of his property; he is arrested by the town council for his pains. From the time of Diocletian (A.D. 284–305) and Constantine (A.D. 306–37) municipal office is the duty of a hereditary caste of *curiales*, who have lost most of their old functions to imperial officials but are jointly held responsible for the collection of taxes and for provisioning the town. In these conditions there could be no civic sense: but there was no easy escape. A member of the curial order was forbidden to leave his native town under the penalty of performing the obligations of both his old home and his new; he might not retire to his country estate to avoid municipal duties; and he was forbidden to enter the army or imperial service, take holy orders, join a guild, or enter into the service of a wealthy proprietor either as personal servant or as tenant farmer. To circumvent any of these devices the obligations of the *curiales*, like those of the guildsmen, were attached to the estate and not to the individual; they were hereditary along with it and there were laws to safeguard the duties in the case of an heiress marrying outside the order in her own town. Eventually enrolment in the curial order became a punishment. Under Maxentius (A.D. 306–12) we hear of Christians being compulsorily enrolled 'to punish them for their superstition'. Constantine (A.D. 306–37) consigned to the order the sons of veterans who would normally have been liable for military service, but who had mutilated themselves to escape it; and towards the end of the fourth century, despite repeated laws forbidding the misuse of the curial order as a legal penalty, Honorius (A.D. 393–423) imposed it on apostate Christians. Under Justinian it is invoked in the Eastern Empire against Jews, heretics and clerics repeatedly convicted of dicing.

True, the measures of compulsion just described were frequently evaded.[1] Both the strident repetitiveness of the codes and a quantity of other evidence shows that the inefficiency of the authorities allowed many fish to slip through the net and that despite the laws there was a good deal of practical mobility and freedom of action. But even when it was successful (as it cannot always have been) the perpetual struggle to evade the law must clearly have carried with it an intolerable burden of anxiety and uncertainty and it is hardly strange that life in these conditions was accompanied by a decline in both the quality and extent of urban civilization. To this the barbarian invasions contributed. In Gaul, especially, where open towns had grown and prospered for generations behind the defences of the Rhine frontier, the enemy ran riot through the province, burning and plundering, once these defences were down. In the general destruction the commercial elements and small artisans seem to have almost entirely disappeared. After the revolt of Postumus against Gallienus (A.D. 259) the towns, with their populations reduced, sank into fortresses, and from the time of Aurelian's reign (A.D. 270–5) onwards it is rare for their area to exceed seventy acres. Thus Bordeaux is exceptionally large with its perimeter of 2,275 metres and an area of seventy-five acres; at Strasbourg the new fortress covers forty-eight acres, Nantes, Rouen and Troyes have each forty, Beauvais, Rennes and Tours twenty-five, and Senlis a mere seventeen. Especially noteworthy is the case of Autun, which covered five hundred acres before it fell to the Gallic armies of

---

1. R. MacMullen, *Journal of Roman Studies*, 1964, pp. 49–53, produces valuable evidence showing that the regulations recorded in the Theodosian code, restricting guildsmen, *curiales* and *coloni*, were in practice often circumvented or even ignored with impunity.

Tetricus, and was pillaged by the Bagaudae, but was rebuilt by Constantius, with the aid of a *corvée* of British carpenters and masons, on a site of only twenty-five acres. Across the Channel, however, the condition of the towns was only a little better. At Verulamium (St. Albans) the city walls fell into ruins and the theatre ceased to be used; and much of Wroxeter was burnt and never rebuilt. Nor was the picture very different in other parts of the Empire. The raids of barbarians into the Balkan peninsula during the third century A.D. reduced its towns to a plight even worse than those of Gaul; and in the safe province of Egypt it is estimated that by A.D. 260 Alexandria had lost some 60 per cent of her former population.

In some instances, notably Strasbourg, it appears that the civilians lived outside the fortress and fell back on it in time of need. But this was exceptional; and in general these figures must imply a considerable decline in population. The remedy—though hardly one which helped the towns—was to continue the practice of settling barbarians within the Empire. We have already traced the beginnings of this policy (above, pp. 64–5). In the third century we hear of Chamavi and Frisii being established behind the frontier, and Constantine (A.D. 306–37) followed the same policy in relation to the Franks. During the fourth century barbarians were introduced in still greater numbers and settled under prefects. Even today many a French village, a Bourgogne, an Alain, or a Sermaize, betrays its origin in the influx of some groups of Burgundians, Alans or Sarmatians. Meanwhile inside the towns any vigorous independent life was being crushed, not merely by the pressure of external events, but also by the increase in bureaucratic control. We have watched the early stages of the process (above, pp. 63–4). By the third century most of the legislative powers of the municipalities had been absorbed by Rome, and the administrative functions were also gradually being usurped. The *curatores* and *correctores* of the third century did their work in bringing all parts of the Empire down to the same dull level of dependence. They were succeeded in the fourth and fifth by the all-powerful *defensor*, who soon came to overshadow all other officials, and often fell into disrepute through his unholy alliance with the local landowners. By this time, of course, the town council was a body possessing only duties, and no real authority.

It has been said with justice that the history of Graeco-Roman civilization is the history of the cities; and countless inscriptions from the first two centuries of the Empire show that for the majority of its citizens it was the city first and foremost which commanded their allegiance and loyalty. Now the most typical institution of ancient civilization was in decay. The middle class of the towns, who had carried Greek and Roman culture to the Tyne and the Indus, to the Tagus and the Dnieper; who had peopled the steppes of Bactria and the river-valleys of France with a constellation of cities, each a replica of the older centres of Greece and Italy, each, let us in fairness admit, a hive of industry and useful activity as well as a centre exploiting the lower classes and the peasants of the surrounding countryside; the urban middle class, who, for all their faults (and they were many), had been the instrument of nearly everything that we value most today in classical civilization—the Attic drama, the histories of Herodotus, Thucydides and Polybius, the sculptures and the temples of Greece, the first eager groping after scientific concepts, the speculations of Plato, Aristotle and Epicurus, the verse of Catullus and Virgil, the noble epic of Lucretius, the satire of Tacitus and Juvenal, the triumphs of Roman architecture and the majestic structure of Roman Law—were now in retreat before the demands of their own creature, the Imperial State.

In these conditions the middle classes had no choice but to fight a rear-guard action. Crushed between the upper and nether mill-stones of the State and an intractable proletariat or peasantry, they felt themselves gradually squeezed out of existence; and their last struggle 'for what remained of political and spiritual freedom against the constraints of tyranny and dogma'[1] has aroused the sympathy and sentiment of modern historians. This sympathy is easily shared. But we should not allow it to obscure our appreciation of what the Emperors achieved. It has been suggested that the dilemma could have been averted, had Septimius Severus not given way to the army by instituting the *annona militaris*; but that is to ignore the key position which the army held in the conditions of the third century, and the need to ensure its loyalty. After all, the invasions of the third century were repelled, and the collapse of

1. Oertel in *Cambridge Ancient History*, Vol. XII, p. 268.

the west postponed for another two centuries. So much must be set to the credit of men who, shrinking from no method, however oppressive, succeeded by an almost superhuman effort in bringing the State through the crisis of the third century, and with it the heritage of Greece and Rome. Cribbed, cabined and confined, something of the classical world still lived on, to penetrate and modify every feature of the later western world that grew up on its ruins. Judged in the light of history, the later emperors performed an essential task and they performed it with great single-mindedness; in its accomplishment lay 'the one last hope of all friends of civilization.'[1]

The characteristic constituent of the world they shaped was compulsion. It was a world in which the lower ranks of society were pressed into a service which sought to regulate their every movement. Concessions to individuals became monopolies for guilds; and guilds rapidly hardened into castes. In A.D. 301 Diocletian attempted to fix prices and maximum wages throughout the Empire, with the death penalty for any breach of his edict. His object was expressly to give further relief to the soldiers, who, though their main needs were satisfied through the *annona militaris*, were still liable 'in a single purchase to be deprived of bonus and salary'. The edict was a failure. Lactantius tells us that goods were withdrawn from the market, that prices rose still more, and that in the end there was 'great bloodshed on account of small and petty details'. But that such an edict should have been introduced is an indication of the extent to which economic and political life was dominated by the idea of compulsion. The world of free exchange and *laissez-faire* was officially dead.

Besides regimenting and controlling, the Emperors also took more positive steps to supplement the failure and decay of private enterprise. Increasingly, the State itself began to enter into the industrial field; for by the beginning of the third century it was no longer possible to distinguish between the Emperor's economic activity as a private individual and direct participation by the State in commerce and industry. For some time the State (or Emperor) had been the largest landowner: now it became the largest owner of mines and quarries and the greatest industrialist. Originally it had entered industry to supply its own needs; the Rhine frontier provides examples of army-potteries at Xanten and Neuss, and at

1. F. M. Heichelheim, *op. cit.* (on p. 23 n. 2) Vol. I, p. 772.

Weisenau near Mainz. Similarly mints, builders' yards, textile mills, iron foundries and armourers' workshops had been established to meet the demands of the court and, more especially, the army. Now, in the fourth and perhaps even in the later part of the third century, imperial factories were set up to supplement the use of controlled private enterprise. The individual works were under procurators responsible, in the West, to a Count of the Imperial Treasury stationed at Rome; their actions were subjected to the most careful scrutiny. We hear of weaving mills, linen mills, works for embroidery in silk and golden thread, dyeworks and ordnance factories. The location of the factories in Illyria, Italy, Gaul, Carthage and Winchester in Britain, seems to have been determined by their proximity to raw materials and their convenience as bases for equipping the armies; and they were evidently meant to satisfy the needs of the army and civil service, not to produce for the market. Some doubts have been expressed whether these institutions were factories in the modern sense, that is, concentrations of workers under a single roof, or whether they were merely collections of hand workers employed in their own homes on conditions imposed by the authorities. There is some evidence that the cottage system was used in the employment of weavers and mint-workers in fourth century Cyzicus. But it would be clearly unwise to generalize from this one example; and in favour of the view that we are dealing with genuine factories is the fact that the work in them, which was difficult and unpopular, was carried out increasingly by forced labour, which would require careful supervision. The dye-works in particular, where the raw materials included human urine and ancient and decayed shell-fish, were largely manned by convicts and slaves; indeed the law frequently imposed forced labour in the mills as a punishment for malefactors. By an edict of A.D. 365, published at Milan, any free-born woman marrying a textile slave must herself take over the occupation of weaver, unless she had declared her free status before marriage. In general one can detect a tendency to try to make the status of both members of guilds and employees in the imperial factories unchangeable and hereditary. For instance, an edict of A.D. 380 forbade the children of workers in the mint to marry outside their own class and as a safeguard against escape such mint-workers were branded on the arm. Similarly the legal Codes are full of penalties for those who conceal runaway textile workers.

Like the troops, these workers received their wages in kind. In the ordnance factories the hands were in fact treated as a semi-militarized corps, and this was also true of the baggage-carriers, who were in charge of bringing up military supplies. Such State employees were thus considerably less independent than even the guildsmen, and Eusebius, without any sense of incongruity, could describe textile hands as 'slaves of the treasury'.

This predominance of the State over the individual and his interests was in essence a reversion to oriental, Bronze Age methods of economic organization. But—and this is important for an understanding of the issue—it was in no sense due to the application of a set of principles. The Emperors did not enter the economic field because they believed in State enterprise; their regulations were not the expression of an ideology favouring regimentation and state control. Hence it is misleading to see the issue as one of principle, as an ideological conflict between the State and the individual. On the contrary, the later Caesars were the victims of circumstances, if ever men were. They found themselves faced with certain problems of finance and essential production, which could be solved in one way and one way only; and they went that way.

NOTES FOR FURTHER READING

There is no full study of the guild organization and development in English. The standard work is J. P. Waltzing, *Étude historique sur les corporations professionelles chez les Romains depuis les origines jusqu'à la chute de l'Empire de l'Occident*, four volumes, Louvain, 1895–1900. See also the article on 'collegium' by E. Kornemann in Pauly-Wissowa's *Real-Encyclopädie der classischen Altertumswissenschaft*, Vol. IV, 1 (1900), cols. 380–480. On the development of the municipalities see F. F. Abbott and A. C. Johnson, *Municipal Administration in the Roman Empire*, Princeton, 1926, containing a valuable collection of original documents, and two books by A. H. M. Jones, *The Greek City from Alexander to Justinian*, Oxford, 1940, and *Cities of the Eastern Roman Provinces*, Oxford, 1937; also an article by C. E. Van Sickle, *Journal of Roman Studies*, 1938, pp. 9 ff., 'Diocletian and the decline of the Roman municipalities'. The text of Diocletian's *Edict on Prices* is published by E. R. Graser in Tenney Frank's *Economic Survey of Ancient Rome*, Vol. V, pp. 305–421; on some later fragments see the same author in *Trans. of the American Philol. Association*, LXXI, 1940, pp. 157–74. Still more new fragments are now available: see I. W. Macpherson, *Journal of Roman Studies*, 1952, p. 72; J. Bingen, *Bulletin de Correspondance Hellénique*, 1954, p. 349; G. Caputo and R. Goodchild, *Journal of Roman Studies*, 1955, pp. 106–15.

6

THE ECONOMY OF THE LATE EMPIRE

AS we have already seen, one expression of the general crisis of
the economic structure was the deterioration of the currency. After the drop in the silver content of the *denarius* to
50 per cent under Septimius Severus (A.D. 193–211) until the reign
of Gallienus (A.D. 253–68) the metal ratio between silver and gold,
and the purchasing power of the coinage, seem to have remained
steady, though gradually more alloy was introduced into the silver.
But after A.D. 256 the quality of the silver coins deteriorated so
rapidly that they were very soon no more than silver-washed
bronze. Diocletian attempted to re-establish the currency with
new silver and gold pieces; the *aureus* weighing $\frac{1}{60}$ of a pound
was equivalent to 24 *argentei*, each $\frac{1}{96}$ of a pound. Meanwhile
silver-washed bronze continued to circulate, and in the *Edict on
Prices*, published in A.D. 301, a pound of gold is valued at 50,000
denarii, which gives an *aureus*: *denarius* ratio of 1: 833·3.

Constantine struck a new gold coin, the *solidus*, weighing
$\frac{1}{72}$ of a pound, and maintained Diocletian's *argenteus*. This system, with minor modifications, which were perhaps intended to
compensate for changes in the relative values of the two metals,
was maintained throughout the fourth century and beyond;
indeed the *solidus* continued to be minted virtually without
change until A.D. 1070, when debased specimens began to appear.
It has been argued that the *solidus* was not a true coin, since it was
weighed in commercial transactions or when paid into the
treasury—Constantine appointed a *zygostates* or official weigher in
each city—and any deficiency of weight made up in small change.
But this argument will not bear examination, since the same was
true of English sovereigns paid into the Bank of England between
A.D. 1816 and 1889, a period when the sovereign was unquestion-
ably a coin in the full sense of the word.

Meanwhile, however, bronze or silvered bronze continued to
decline in value, perhaps because the government, concerned only
with its own fiscal advantage, went on issuing more and more
while insisting on having its taxes paid only in gold or in *natura*.

The ratio between the *denarius*, now merely a notional sum, a fraction of the smallest bronze coin, and the *solidus* was constantly changing to the detriment of the former. Evidence from Egyptian papyri shows that in A.D. 324 the *solidus* was worth 4,350 *denarii* in Egypt; it rapidly fell to 54,000, to 150,000, to 180,000 and by about A.D. 338 was equivalent to 257,000. Just over ten years later it was worth 5,760,000 *denarii* and by the later years of the century 45,000,000. If in the west the figures appear less catastrophic, that is perhaps because the word *denarius* was there used for the *nummus* or bronze coin, and not for its notional subdivision.

At first sight such an inflation might be expected to have put an end to all normal economic life based on a money economy. But this was not so. Naturally commodities tended to rise in price in terms of the currency that was being debased; for example, we find the price of a loaf of bread at Ephesus doubling between the reign of Trajan and the decade A.D. 220–30. Moreover in any inflation wages tend to lag behind prices, and this would of course add to the economic distress. On the other hand, a modern inflation in which notes are multiplied results in a fall in the value of all notes, new and old: but the debasing of silver only affects the new coins, which therefore tend to be retariffed, leaving the older specimens untouched. In fact, inscriptions make a sharp distinction between 'old coins' and 'new'. Hoarded money—and hoarding was among the commonest forms of saving in ancient times—maintained its value; and the main loss was sustained by people who had lent large sums with an agreement for fixed repayments, and by those who had the misfortune to accept the new coins before the new rate was established. Inflation introduced an element of uncertainty into business dealings, and the effects of this can be traced. But after each fall in the silver content of the *denarius* there was a period of stability, during which commerce went on as usual; and at no time did money disappear from economic life.

To a considerable extent, it is true, we find guild members working for a pittance or even a financial loss, and receiving recompense largely in kind; and the army and state employees generally were on a similar footing. But another sector of the economy, and that by no means negligible, still operated by means of money. For example, payment of taxes in kind only applied to those living on the land; for others there were taxes in gold and silver. Thus senators, in addition to the *annona* levied on their estates, were liable for a special surtax, and also for the payment of a sum of gold on the occasion of the emperor's accession and each five-yearly anniversary of it; with the multiplication of emperors this could become a very considerable impost. Likewise the magistrates and council-members of the various cities were required to contribute 'crown gold', theoretically in celebration of special occasions and later, after A.D. 364, as a compulsory donation. Finally, the trading classes, including virtually anyone who pursued a gainful employment, were liable for a special tax, levied every five years on the capital involved in a business, with a minimum payment for those whose capital was negligible. This tax, which had to be paid in gold and silver, and was consequently called the *chrysargyrum*, went to pay for imperial shows and army donations; it weighed heavily on the city-dwellers, and Libanius speaks of parents driven to enslave or prostitute their children to find the necessary sum.

With the exception of the *annona* all these taxes were paid in metal, and with the proceeds Constantine minted his gold coinage. Moreover, even the *annona* did not remain a tax exacted purely in kind. As early as A.D. 213 in Egypt, but to a much greater extent in the course of the fourth century, it had begun to evolve into yet one more tax in gold. Gradually the custom grew up of commuting the obligations of the tax into a payment in gold, a process known as *adaeratio*, and the same substitution also appears in the paying of government employees. The government at first resisted; and various rescripts forbade the practice. But with the general growth of stability it made headway, and in A.D. 364 and 365 it was permitted in the payment of certain state employees, including soldiers along the Danube frontier. Twenty years later it was accepted as a general practice in Illyricum; and in the course of the fifth century it was made compulsory in the payment of officials, and appears to be recommended for the army. Finally in A.D. 439 it was adopted for troops and civil service alike, and in the west at least the period of state payments in kind was at an end. This development was not completed without difficulties. In particular, complications arose concerning the rate at which the conversion was to be calculated—for example in the case of swine due to be paid in Southern Italy, whether the rate at Rome or that in the local market should be the basis of the commutation. Again, who was to bear the cost of transporting the animals to the capital? This is but one example of the difficulties that arose in the clash of interests between army and civil service on the one hand, landowners on the other, and the government collectors between the two. Gradually these problems were surmounted with the institution of seasonal tariffs fixed by the praetorian prefects, and it was possible to abandon the tax in kind, though commodities continued to be the basis on which the obligation in gold was calculated.

It is thus clear that a money economy was never completely effaced during the third and fourth centuries. For this we have the evidence of Diocletian's *Edict on Prices* and various papyri, and also the writings of the Church Fathers, who consistently assume the operation of a full money economy; we read of landowners profiting by scarcity and fearing a good harvest, sure signs of a market, of craftsmen working on their own account or as wage-earners for others, and of active retail trade in everyday articles and foodstuffs, all employing money. Moreover the remarkable operation carried out by the rich and pious Melania who, in the early years of the fifth century, sold all her estates scattered over the western provinces for 120,000 *solidi*, and distributed this sum in alms to the poor, would have been economically impossible under a system of barter.

In short, despite the apparent state control of all undertakings throughout the fourth and early fifth centuries, a good deal of the economic life of the provinces continued to be in the hands of small men. In so far as these small men worked for themselves or for wages, they used money. But it was, as a rule, the debased silver and bronze of the inflations, and the amount available varied from time to time and from province to province. Minting was carried out with an eye on the army and its needs, not on private trade; thus Spain had to rely on South Gaul for its currency, and with one brief exception Africa had to obtain its coinage from Italy. Even in those provinces well supplied with money, the gold *solidus* was too large for everyday transactions. It is not until the time of Theodosius (A.D. 379–95) that small coins appear in the precious metals; and by now the stresses and wars in many parts of the west were too acute to permit of full recovery. The fourth century silver hoards of Britain (which possessed no mint except during the years A.D. 296–324, when there was one at London) point to a shortage of gold; and after A.D. 400 small coins disappear completely from both Britain and the Danube area. Throughout the west the economy was much enfeebled, and in this part of the Empire, from Diocletian's time onwards, two economies seem to have existed side by side. For the general population, including the army and the state employees, there were public distributions of the necessities of life, supplemented by wages in the debased bronze currency for the purchase of small additional trifles on the free market. Simultaneously, though silver ceased to be minted by the fifth century, the rich enjoyed the advantages of a good gold coinage, with which they could buy every kind of luxury from all parts of the known world.

These conclusions are confirmed by the picture which has survived of trade in the later Empire. Recently discovered fragments of Diocletian's *Edict on Prices*, which give the rates for sea transport for some fifty-seven specified trips between five named ports in the eastern half of the Empire and every part of the Mediterranean, show that sea traffic was, unlike land transport, still reasonably cheap. According to these tariffs, which are a fair reflection of conditions at the beginning of the fourth century, it was possible to ship a cargo of wheat the whole length of the Mediterranean, from Asia to Western Spain, for 26 per cent of its maximum value. Accordingly, the *Edict* presupposes a very considerable trade in objects of ordinary use of inter-provincial dimensions.

One must not, however, imagine this to have been on the same scale as the trade of the early Principate. The evidence is sporadic and often unreliable; but what there is points to a very marked regression, especially in the western provinces. Gaul still produced textiles, wool and linen; and in the glass industry, indeed, it advanced beyond anything achieved in the early Empire. Technical improvements in the second century had resulted in a fine transparent glass, frequently adorned with pictorial or mythological themes, and manufactured at various sites in Bourbonnais, Poitou, Vendée, Loire-Inférieure, Argonne, Eifel, and especially Cologne. During the third century this industry, like all others, suffered severely from uncertain conditions, and the invasions and social distress; but Constantine and his successors encouraged its recovery with special concessions to glass and filigree workers, provided that they undertook to pass on their skill to their children. As a result, the glass trade continued to flourish throughout the fourth century, serving the court at Trier, the nearby army, and the Gallic aristocracy. Glassware was not however used by the peasants and small artisans and traders, and though some was exported to Asia and Scandinavia, it remained a luxury and the industry never reached the scale achieved by the earlier potteries. Moreover, from the late fourth century there is a regression in quality.

This decline is part of a general trend and is to be seen in the gradual disappearance of the guilds. Under the early Empire Gallic shippers were found in every port; in the fourth century we have records of shippers from Africa, Spain and Egypt, but none from Gaul; and the new fragments of Diocletian's *Edict* suggest that the domination of the shipping trade by easterners was already beginning. The river transport guilds, which flourished earlier, have also disappeared; whether their activities have been transferred to the nationalized services and the militarized flotillas of the lakes and rivers of France and Switzerland is uncertain.

Further east in Germany and the Danube provinces there was a late flowering of an economy largely based on the army and the frontier trade. But it became increasingly the imperial policy to restrict the latter. First iron and bronze, then gold, were placed on the list of objects which might not be exported to the barbarians. Trade of any kind must pass through certain specified frontier posts; and very soon we find arms, wine, corn, oil, and even fish sauce included among the commodities which might not cross the border. This policy of restriction, which was largely imposed by motives of defence, killed what trade was beginning to grow up; and in A.D. 413, when the court was moved from Trier to Arles, the economy of the north suffered a fatal blow. Deserted by the rich, who fled south taking what they could, these areas deteriorated to a level not very different from that across the German frontier. On the other hand Britain experienced a St. Martin's summer in the fourth century, when the upper classes in their villas enjoyed a burst of vulgar prosperity, with mass-produced objects of both continental and native manufacture. But in general the trend, as elsewhere, was towards local self-sufficiency for articles of mass consumption. The villas reveal few foreign objects, and the impression is one of quiet comfort until imperial neglect and the withdrawal of the legions opened up the province to the invading Saxons.

Spain also enjoyed a modest prosperity up to the early fourth century. There was a good deal of road construction and internal trade carried on by hawkers and pedlars; and even in the fourth century Ausonius in Gaul was receiving gifts of olive oil and the still famous fish sauce from Barcelona. In A.D. 324 and 336 corn was sent from Spain to Rome. But the decline in the amount of evidence reflects economic decay; there is a shortage of currency— Spain had no mint—and the general picture becomes increasingly obscure. Sicily remained a land of primary production, with large estates and ranches, and some profit from the tourist traffic. For senators, who were forbidden at this time to travel elsewhere, might go to Sicily. Africa, until its seizure by the Vandals (A.D. 429–39), remained a storehouse for Rome. Carthage was still a prosperous city. But the manning of the quarries was already a serious problem by the third century, and in general the country seems never to have recovered from the pillaging which followed the suppression of the Gordian revolt in A.D. 238. In the fourth century life was considerably disturbed by the activities of the *circumcelliones*, bands of wandering supporters of the Donatist schism, who indulged in the violence of a movement which united religious, social and perhaps nationalist strands; their opposition to Rome eventually led them to give support to the invading Vandals.

Italy, meanwhile, had continued to decline. In the fourth century vast tracts of land were out of cultivation, and brigandage so common that in A.D. 364 the use of horses was forbidden to shepherds and even landowners in seven provinces. By the end of the century half a million *iugera*—more than a quarter of a million acres—were lying fallow in the once smiling land of Campania; and in A.D. 450 the legal codes refer to children sold into slavery because of the starvation of their parents. For several centuries now Italy had played a passive role in imperial commerce. It no longer aimed at doing more than satisfying some of its own needs. Indeed from the time of Diocletian onwards the part of the peninsula south of the Rubicon was released from the payment of *annona*, on condition of its supplying Rome with meat, wine, wood and lime. Here as elsewhere the guilds were subordinated more and more to the needs of the State. But with the Gothic invasions of the fifth century and the cessation of corn imports from Vandal Africa, records became meagre and difficult to interpret. The evidence points to the disappearance of the guilds, and the whole organization of which they formed a part, with the collapse of the western Empire in A.D. 476.

Until the general break-up in the fifth century, money continued to be employed throughout the western provinces; and with the adoption of *adaeratio* in all fields the fiscal experiment of collecting the taxes and paying the army and civil service to a large extent in kind came to an end. Nevertheless, particularly in the West, where towns were more recent and less frequent, this experiment had helped to consolidate a trend by no means negligible among the causes of the final disruption of the State.

As we saw, the pressure on the small man, on the guildsman and the independent peasant, the danger from the troops themselves, and the often insupportable burden of taxation and pressed labour, led more and more of the victims to take to flight; and it often happened that there was only one refuge—the large and powerful landowner. For the landlords survived and even prospered when the city men perished or, if they could escape their obligations as *curiales*, withdrew to their estates and themselves became exclusively landlords. Moreover it is a mark of the primacy of land as the chief economic factor in the ancient world that the 'racketeers' who naturally sprang up under the bureaucracy and in the chaos of the third century—men who flourished

not so much by virtue of their commercial ability and business energy, as the old bourgeoisie had done, but rather by unscrupulousness, extortion, bribery and the exploitation of the political constellation of the moment[1]

—put their wealth, not, like the Goerings and Cianos of the twentieth century, into industry, but into land. Instead of industrial monopolists they became feudal barons; and in an age in which a strongly centralized government could be influenced only by the exertion of group pressures, it is noteworthy that the great landowners constituted the most effective and powerful of such groups,

1. Oertel in *Cambridge Ancient History*, Vol. XII, p. 274.

more influential even than the army or the church and outstripped in this respect only by the highest members of the civil service, the lawyers and the senatorial aristocracy (who were, of course, often identical with them). By contrast the peasantry, freeholders and tenants alike, and the craftsmen, shopkeepers and merchants of the towns had no way of expressing their grievances or swaying policy in a direction favourable to their interests. Indeed, if one is to understand this age, one must draw a sharp distinction between the small man bound to his strict routine by bureaucratic codes and police sanctions and the extravagant lives of successful careerists. There is a good deal of truth in an apparently paradoxical description of the declining years of the western Empire, with their lack of any real social ethic, as an age of dreary individualism.[1]

The manor economy which thus grew up and flourished played an important cultural part in the history of the later Empire. As the towns decayed, the manors produced for the local market; and in this way the new, mediaeval orientation of the countryside towards the manor and its owner becomes more marked, and the relationship between the latter and the surrounding district intensified. Moreover, the manors were the chief remaining market for the international luxury trade, which continued to operate even after all primary needs were being satisfied locally. The rich landowners had the means to pay for spices from the east, elaborate woods and precious stones, which not being bulky still amply repaid the risks entailed in their shipment. Such manor houses, homes of luxury and culture even in the darkest hours of the Empire, stand out as the new guardians of the ancient tradition; and to some extent they bring culture to the countryside, with which they enjoy a more intimate relationship than was ever possible for the towns, whose place they have taken. A dissemination of culture at an infinitely lower level than had existed in the cities, but over a far wider area, was perhaps one of the more important positive achievements of this period.

Economically too the manorial household succeeded in bridging a gap which the classical economy had never managed to close—that between peasant proprietorship and the capitalistic plantation worked by slave labour. As we saw, slavery was at this time a declining institution. Not that it disappeared entirely.

1. A. H. M. Jones, *The Greek City*, 303; cf. *The Later Roman Empire*, I, 357–65, for an analysis of pressure groups.

The barbarian wars of the fourth century opened up new sources
of supply; and in times of distress there was some recrudescence
of debt-slavery and the sale of infants. Indeed the rich may
still have possessed slaves on what seems a tremendous scale,
if we may judge from Melania, who manumitted 8,000 by a
single act. Yet the slave had declined in importance; and he had
been largely replaced on the land by the tenant-farmer or *colonus*.
Throughout the Empire, as agriculture fell back to subsistence
levels, it became convenient to parcel out large estates among
poor tenants or settlers, who paid the landlord with a fixed proportion of their yield and, in certain provinces (though not in
Italy), with a stipulated amount of labour annually. This labour,
reminiscent of the services exacted from those holding land 'in
free socage' in mediaeval times, was constantly being increased
by the landlord (or, more often, by the rich tenant who came
between the landlord and the *colonus*) with the connivance of the
imperial officials. An African inscription of the second century A.D.
has survived, in which certain tenants, 'rustics of small means,
winning a livelihood by the work of their hands', as they describe
themselves, celebrate an unexpected legal victory in resisting such
a demand.

These small tenants were originally free men, bound only by
their respective contracts. But as early as Nero (A.D. 54–68) we
hear of the transfer of barbarian settlers inside the Empire (see
above, p. 64); and from the time of M. Aurelius (A.D. 161–80) it
became common for the emperors to replenish the depleted fields
of the provinces with German settlers defeated in war. These
tributarii, as they were termed, though for many purposes they
ranked as free men, were legally tied to their plots of land. Not
unnaturally the distinction between the free Roman *colonus* and
the unfree Romanized *tributarius* soon began to be blurred; and
as might be expected, it was the status of the *colonus* which
deteriorated. However, there were more violent forces at work
than mere assimilation. As we saw, Septimius Severus (A.D.
193–211) instituted a new tax, the *annona*, which consisted of a
fixed amount of produce to be provided by landowners; and this
tax was further systematized at the end of the century by
Diocletian, who issued a rescript laying down the quantity of
foodstuffs for the production of which each estate throughout the
Empire was liable, based not only on acreage, but also on the

Transport of wine. Bas-relief from Langres showing a pair of mules drawing a large barrel on a four-wheeled cart. Note the primitive harness and absence of a collar.

Isis Giminiana. This drawing from a fresco from a tomb at Ostia, and now in the Vatican, shows the 'Isis Giminiana', a river craft (*navis codiciaria*) plying between Ostia and Rome, being loaded with grain, which is measured as it is poured into a sack. Farnaces, the ship's captain, stands at the stern.

Bishapur. This shows the victory of the Sassanid king, Sapor I, over the Roman emperor Valerian; the technique parallels that of the reliefs on the Arch of Constantine opposite.

The Arch of Constantine. Erected in Rome in 315 to celebrate the emperor's Christian victory over Maxentius; its carefully worded inscription avoids giving offence to the pagan majority.

Reliefs from the Arch. These show the emperor addressing the people and distributing money; on the oriental influence revealed in the arrangement of the figures see p. 105.

Aurei. The three lower coins are *aurei* struck by Maximian (*b*), Galerius (*c*) and Licinius (*d*); the last shows the emperor standing between two conquered barbarians. The large gold medallion (*a*) shows the emperor Constantine in imperial dress (*obverse*) and standing with a globe and consular sceptre (*reverse*).

a

b

c

d

Sea-going ships. A mosaic from Sousse (Hadrumetum) in N. Africa shows two fast ships, perhaps police boats (*naves tesserariae*).

Landowner fighting Scythians. This mural decoration in a tomb at Panticapaeum (Kerch in the Crimea) shows a fight between a local landowner on horseback (on the left) and a band of Scythian marauders.

'heads of male labour' employed, no matter what their legal status. Thus from the beginning of the third century onwards it became a matter of imperial policy to support the landlord in any measures he might take to ensure that his fields were adequately cultivated, and the fiscal demands of the government satisfied. Under the pressure of bad harvests and consequent debt the *colonus*—as we have seen—was apt to take refuge in flight. Consequently at some date during the third century—perhaps in consequence of a census carried out by Diocletian, though unfortunately the evidence does not allow of chronological precision—the attachment of the tenant farmer to the manorial estate was made enforceable at law. In a rescript of Constantine dated 30 October A.D. 332, this situation is clearly defined as already in existence; henceforward any *colonus* who fled was to be brought back in chains like a runaway slave.

Once established, the principle of compulsion in reference to land tenure grew rapidly. In the third century we still read of *inquilini*, men domiciled on the estates but free to move; but in the course of the fourth century they too were tied to the land and reduced to effective serfdom. By A.D. 400 the legal codes speak of the peasants as *servi terrae*, virtually slaves of the land on which they were born. More and more they are oppressed in the interests of their former landlords, now their masters; and a stream of legislation defines ever more closely the terms of their subjection.

The Emperors viewed this growth in the power of the landlords with mixed feelings. It placed them in a dilemma. They might attempt to enrol the landlords in the service of the State by such regulations as that of Valens (A.D. 364–78), which made them responsible for the collection of all the taxes for which their *coloni* were liable. At the same time it was recognized that the growth of the landlords was essentially a symptom of the breakdown of the State. Everywhere the colonate was constantly being recruited from the ranks of the independent peasants, whom hard times drove to throw themselves on the mercy of the local landlord, surrendering their freedom in exchange for his patronage and protection. In A.D. 368 this practice was declared illegal by the same emperor Valens, who thus sought simultaneously to check and utilize an inevitable but ultimately disruptive institution. In fact the great landlords throve against the State and usurped its functions. Thus we find them along the northern frontiers, or in Africa, raising private armies of slaves—forerunners of the Mamelukes and Janissaries of the Ottoman Empire—to carry out frontier defence, and expelling the barbarian alone. But in the long run, by weakening the central authority, the manorial system weakened defence too, and especially in the western provinces it accelerated the disruption of the Empire. Meanwhile it helped in the general process by which the population of the Empire crystallized into the various social classes, each with its duties carefully defined in the new body of legislation which sprang up to give full sanction to the authoritarian state.

These gradings, which form the essence of the later mediaeval world, begin to appear during the first three centuries A.D., and find their full legal authority in the fourth. The old categories of *cives Romani*, freedmen, slaves and the like, no longer exist. Instead, the whole population of the Empire is divided into *honestiores*, who include the Emperor, the (Christian) priesthood and the new landed proprietors, together with officers, civil servants and the few big families of the towns, and *humiliores*, who include ultimately everyone else, whether serf or slave, craftsman or peasant. For these two grades there are separate functions, separate privileges and separate punishments; the antagonism of the classes has once more reached its logical end in the artificial creation of two different kinds of human being.

This structure, stable, simplified and primitive, was what came out of the Empire. Under this system the legacy of the ancient world was transmitted to later times. Meanwhile the real classical world had perished in the west. At the end of the fourth century the Danubian troops were disbanded because there was no longer any paymaster; and in the fifth century it proved impossible to raise even the small armies of ten to twenty thousand men necessary to repel the barbarians. The invasions thus met with little real resistance in a world already torn within, decentralized and irreparably weakened both socially and economically. As we can see from Salvian's imprecations, men lost faith in the Empire, in its justice and in its righteousness, even if they still assumed its continued existence as a matter of habit. We hear of men taking refuge with the barbarians, and of others who gave them aid and encouragement as they penetrated the Roman provinces. Thus a few thousand barbarians were enough to push over this tottering edifice. Meanwhile the setting-up of a new capital at Byzantium in A.D. 330 had meant the virtual division of the Empire, though this was not made absolute until the death of Theodosius the Great in A.D. 395. In A.D. 410 Alaric the Visigoth sacked Rome; and in A.D. 476 Odoacer liquidated a bankrupt concern by deposing Romulus Augustulus, the last western Emperor.

In the east the Empire continued to exist as a bulwark of Christendom until A.D. 1453, though after the reign of Justinian (A.D. 527–65) it fell on days almost as evil as those which had destroyed the west. As in the western provinces, barbarians penetrated its boundaries, and in the Balkans the Latin and Greek populations were largely diluted by Slavs. Nevertheless, behind the fortifications of Constantine's new capital, the central government maintained its power and its continuity. Why it survived when the west collapsed is a problem not easy to resolve; for many of the symptoms of decline were common to both halves of the Empire. But an important factor seems to be that the destruction of the middle classes of the cities, and the growth of a landed aristocracy, with interests distinct from and often opposed to those of the court, is much less apparent in the east.

There were of course great landowners; but they were partly held in check by the preservation of a free peasantry which, after a long struggle, succeeded in hindering its depression to the level of the western *colonus*. Nor were they permitted to take the same share in the government as the landlords of the west. The taxes continued to be collected by public officials, not by the landed gentry. The onset of feudalism was thus postponed. In short, the centre of gravity remained much closer to the towns, and there was less scope for the setting up of a purely rural economy. In addition, the east was more populous than the west, and its military reservoir of semi-civilized manpower in the hills of Asia Minor gave it great advantages in the dark days of barbarian invasion. Nor should we neglect the existence of Constantinople itself, a fortress at the very core of the eastern Empire, hard to take and capable of extending its aid wherever required. Lastly, as has been pointed out,[1] the eastern Emperors, because of these factors, were able to keep the wheels of the imperial machine turning, and so to collect the taxes and maintain both the army along the frontiers and the civil administration within them.

1. N. H. Baynes, *Journal of Roman Studies*, 1943, 24–25.

However, with the eastern Empire we are not directly concerned. Its achievements were far from negligible; but they lay
largely in the field of preservation and in the maintenance of
equilibrium, or else in a religious sphere quite alien to the tradition
of classical Greece and Rome. To say this is not to belittle what
Byzantium saved and what she created. The question recently
raised in Toynbee's *Study of History*, whether Byzantium should be
regarded as the true continuation of the Roman Empire, or as a
'successor-state' similar to the Gothic kingdoms or Charlemagne's empire in the west, is ultimately one of terminology.
There was continuity and there was also some degree of change.
Justinian, the codifier of Roman Law, took an important step to
further commerce when he introduced silk manufacture from the
far east; and from the sixth to the eleventh century Byzantium
remained the greatest trading power in Christendom. Yet throughout these centuries the legacy of the Roman Empire, as we have
analysed it, was palpably clear. Byzantium remained a caste-state,
with many of its rural districts desolate and its agriculture feeble,
with neither the economic foundations nor the mental atmosphere
to conceive and carry through any radical social change. It was a
portent for the new relations of east and west when in A.D. 1204
Constantinople fell to the marauders of the Fourth Crusade, who
held it till A.D. 1265. In A.D. 1453, with the capture of the city by
the Turks, the Eastern Empire at last came to an end. By this time
its work of preservation was done. The very rise of its trade rivals
in the cities of Italy, which largely contributed to its decay and
finally undermined its century-long resistance, at the same time
signified that the main stream of progress was once more advancing
in the west.

NOTES FOR FURTHER READING

See the books mentioned already after Chapters III–V. The problem of the
currency and the inflation is best treated by the Finnish scholar G. Mickwitz,
Geld und Wirtschaft im römischen Reich des IV. Jahrhunderts (Comm. hum.
litt. IV, 2), Helsinki, 1932. This fundamental study deals with the question
of *adaeratio* and the extent to which there was a reversion to natural economy;
it is modified in some details by A. Passerini in the book mentioned after
Chapter IV. See also S. Bolin, *State and Currency in the Roman Empire to
300 A.D.*, Stockholm, 1958, and Piganiol's book, mentioned after Chapter I.
On the general development of this later period see J. B. Bury, *History of*

the Later Roman Empire, ed. 2, London 1923, Vol. I. Details of trade will be found in the various volumes of Frank's *Economic Survey;* see also P. Vinogradoff, *Cambridge Mediaeval History*, Vol. I, ed. 2, 1924, pp. 542–67, with bibliography: 'Social and economic conditions of the Roman Empire in the fourth century', and the present writer's chapter in the *Cambridge Economic History of Europe*, Vol. II, already mentioned after Chapter III. On land conditions see C. E. Stevens' chapter in the same work, Vol. I, and the following articles in the *Real-Encyclopädie: 'colonatus'* by O. Seeck. Vol. IV, 1, cols. 483–510, 'Domänen' by E. Kornemann, in Supplement-Band IV, cols. 227–68. On the survival of Byzantium see Baynes' article quoted after Chapter I, and J. B. Bury, *Quarterly Review*, CXCII, 1900, pp. 129–55, 'Rome and Byzantium'. On the ideological background of the barbarian invasions see P. Courcelle, *Histoire littéraire des grandes invasions germaniques*, ed. 3, Paris, 1964.

7

THE CULTURAL BACKGROUND

GROWTH and decay are processes affecting society through and through; it is unthinkable that they should leave any single one of man's activities—his music, art, religion, literature, thought or language—untouched. Yet the connection between the various fields is never simple, and it by no means follows that decay in one sphere will be accompanied by decay in another. On the contrary, it is here above all that the relativity of change is evident, and with it the need to establish different criteria of growth and decay in each particular sector. Here space does not allow a full survey of these various fields; but no discussion of the nature and causes of the decline of the Western Empire can be satisfactory which does not attempt to trace at least some of its cultural manifestations.

Discussing the mental atmosphere under the Empire, a German scholar describes the third century A.D. in these terms:

As knowledge rapidly sank, there was a pronounced rise in the power of belief and its bastard brother, superstition. In that respect this century is the precise opposite of the third century B.C.—then the high point of exact science, now a revulsion from civilization and a deep yearning to win release from earthly misery through the growing power of the mystery religions . . . In half a millenium antiquity had transformed itself from a world of knowledge into a world of belief; from philosophy it had gone over (since the time of Poseidonius (c. 135–51 B.C.)) to theology, from astronomy to astrology; it was now ripe for a purely hieratic culture.[1]

'There were no free thinkers in those times;' writes a French scholar,[2] 'all men, from the lowest ranks to the summit of society are religious or at least superstitious.' This change in mental outlook, this 'failure of nerve', as J. B. Bury once termed it, is one of the most notable indications of conflict and crisis in the classical era.

The increasing role played by religion, in contrast to the earlier

1. E. Kornemann, *Römische Geschichte* (Vol. III, 2 of Gercke-Norden, *Einleitung in die Altertumswissenschaft*, Leipzig, 1933), p. 93.
2. F. Lot, *Le Fin du monde antique et le début du moyen âge*, Paris, 1927, p. 34.

humanism and confidence in the adequacy of rational thought, is a phenomenon for which no single explanation is sufficient. Beyond doubt, periods of social crisis are reflected in the questionings, longings and general psychological disquiet of ordinary men. 'What people in that century were longing for', writes Charlesworth,[1] in a discussion of the hysterical litanies of the third century A.D., 'was escape, though they hardly knew escape from what.' And this spontaneous search for spiritual succour, amid difficulties which it seemed past the wit of man to solve, found expression in the growth of various religions and superstitions both in Hellenistic times and under the Roman Empire. At the same time one should not ignore the part played by the Roman State, of set policy, in this matter. As early as the fourth century B.C., in describing a utopia which had the aim of maintaining a strictly demarcated class-society in perpetuum, Plato deliberately welcomed and inculcated superstition not only for the lower classes, but even for the wardens of the community. The political view of religion had already been elaborated by the Critias, a relative of Plato, who, towards the end of the fifth century, set up an oligarchy at Athens. To Critias religion was merely the clever invention of some shrewd man who thought that the instilling of the fear of an omniscient god who punished evil-doing would render the task of the governor more easy. Two hundred years later the services which religion could render to political stability were recognized by Polybius, who expressed his admiration for the skill with which the Roman State kept its lower classes in subjection by a judicious compound of terrors and pageantry.

This political function of religion was reckoned high up among the devices adopted by Hellenistic statecraft. The peoples of Greece, Asia Minor, Syria or Egypt were encouraged to satisfy their longings for a 'Saviour', a 'Benefactor' and a 'Liberator' by deifying their various kings under these titles. The practice had old-established roots in the monarchies of Babylonia and Egypt, and came easy to Greeks, who knew how a mortal like Heracles could be raised to heaven. Indeed it would be highly misleading to suggest that the Hellenistic ruler-cult had to be imposed by the kings upon their subjects. On the contrary, the initiative often came from the people themselves, as when the populace of Athens invoked

1. M. P. Charlesworth, 'The "Virtues" of a Roman Emperor' in Proceedings of the British Academy, 1937, pp. 123ff.

the help of the Macedonian Demetrius the Besieger against
Aetolia in these terms:

The other gods are non-existent or afar off; either they do not hear or they
pay no heed: but you, you are here, and we can see you, not in wood nor
in stone, but in very truth.

From the deification of Hellenistic rulers it seemed only a short
step to the bestowal of similar titles on Roman proconsuls, like
Flamininus and Scipio, who in the second century B.C. had equally
shown themselves benefactors to Greece in times of trouble. When
Augustus made himself supreme head of the Roman State in 31 B.C.
he soon discovered the efficacy of deification. Julius Caesar, the
hard-headed politician and general, now dead, had already been
dubbed the 'Divine Julius'; and subsequently it became usual to
deify all Emperors, except those most detested by the ruling class,
upon their deaths, or even beforehand. In addition, as part of his
programme of consolidation, Augustus deliberately gave fresh
emphasis to the old traditional gods, Jupiter, Vesta, Venus, Apollo
and the rest; and he set about the restoration of disused and ruined
temples on a wide scale. In 12 B.C., when he took the office of
Pontifex Maximus (High Priest), he endowed it with a new and
historically significant lease of life. From this moment dated the
bond in Europe between throne and altar.

In Ionia and Athens of the sixth and fifth centuries B.C. there
had been notable technical advances, and speculative science had
reached considerable heights, though hampered by an inadequate
technique of experiment by which its hypotheses might have been
put to the test. Later, applied science made headway at Alexandria.
But the deep social cleft, which drew a line between work of the
hand and work of the mind, created an atmosphere in which science
could no more flourish than democracy. The vacuum which it left
was extended by failure in the social and economic field; and the
Empire became the seed-bed of a multitude of cults, most of
which arose in the ferment of the eastern Mediterranean, and were
carried far and wide along the trade routes of the Empire. While
the upper classes devoted themselves more and more to the
vaguely humanitarian tenets of Stoicism—a philosophy not ill-
adapted to the uncertainties of life in the first century A.D. under
Caligula, Nero or Domitian—the masses sought comfort from the
east. Under the Republic the cults of Isis and the Great Mother had

spread to Italy and attracted a growing number of devotees. But more popular than either were the two religions which began to make headway under the early Empire—the cult of Mithras, identified with the Unconquered Sun, among the soldiers along the frontiers, and Christianity among the city proletariat. It was the latter which for several reasons was ultimately to prevail.

The Christian teaching of a Messiah who would save all believers, and whose return to earth was imminent, had many points in common with the mystery religions, and with such cults as those of Attis and Cybele, Adonis, Dionysus, Isis and Osiris. While it accepted the current belief in devils and witchcraft, which formed part of the common content of thought at this time, being approved even by Stoicism, it corresponded closely to the 'messianic' mood of the masses in the near east and, as a creation of the downtrodden, it spread with the proletarianising of the other classes—this notwithstanding the persecution which it at first suffered, because it refused to share its allegiance with the divine Emperor. The more mundane teachings of Christianity were also adapted to the needs of the poor. Its condemnation of usury was welcomed by a world in the clutches of the ubiquitous money-lender. Moreover, it gained strength from its readiness in practice, if to a less extent in theory, to admit women to a prominent position in its church organisation. As it spread, it shed such genuine revolutionary traits as had characterized its Jewish origins, and with remarkable adaptability acquired instead a Greek philosophical background, a ritual and a theology. Its economic doctrine, as formulated by the early fathers, corresponds exactly with the needs of the stagnating economy of the third-century Empire; its ideal has been described as a modest income and much time for thought, prayer, holy conversation and good works; it puts its hopes, not in this world, but in the next. Indeed the way seems to be opening for a rapprochement between Church and State, when Diocletian begins his famous edict of A.D. 301 regulating prices by enunciating a sentiment typical of the early Church Fathers that 'uncontrolled economic activity is a religion of the godless'. But unity between the two was hindered by the refusal of the Church to compromise; and the persecutions of Diocletian intervened before the movement could be consummated in A.D. 312 by the conversion of Constantine. At last Christianity and the Empire had come to terms, and henceforth the authoritarian state had acquired a new ally, which disguised it under 'a religious veneer, and stamped subjection as resignation to the will of God.'[1] From the time of Diocletian, with Constantine following closely in his footsteps, the elaborate court hierarchy arrayed itself in the borrowed trappings of a religious terminology. Diocletian and Maximian had placed their dynasties under the divine protection of Jupiter and Hercules respectively; and they drew freely upon the outward forms of the Sassanid court, with its oriental ceremonial and eunuchs, diadem, scarlet boots, purple robes and air of sacred mystification. In a Christian Empire the Divine Emperor was necessarily transformed into the Emperor by the Grace of God; but the atmosphere remained unchanged. In the 'Sacred Palace' at Constantinople dwelt the Emperor's 'Divine Household'. A 'Sacred Consistory' acted as his Privy Council; and even his treasury disguised itself as the 'Sacred Benefactions'.

While Christianity was thus providing the Empire with an international creed which could leap frontiers with even greater agility than the doctrine of the Divine Emperor, various occult and irrational beliefs appeared, to solace people in the intolerable conditions of the times. Neoplatonism infused the ancient doctrines of the Academy with an appropriate strain of mysticism, and in Plotinus produced at least one figure fit to stand in the first ranks of ancient philosophy; but the general level was infinitely far below this, and in the virtually nonsensical *Hermetica* men lost all touch with reality. Not only are the findings of ancient science lost, to make way for the most absurd and puerile hypotheses; but, worse still, knowledge no longer matters. The scientific study of the heavens can be neglected, argues St. Ambrose; for wherein does it assist our salvation? Thus the classical curtain went down on a picture which represents the complete disintegration of rational thought.

Roman literature too provides a faithful reflection of the general process of decline; and by its early demise shows conclusively (if proof is still required) that the decay of the Empire was not due to something which happened a little before A.D. 250, but that some of the operative factors were already active centuries before.

1. F. Oertel in *Cambridge Ancient History*, Vol. XII, p. 270.

The sensitive plant of literature was one of the first to succumb, whereas hardier manifestations like architecture and engineering carried on for another two centuries.

The *Pax Augusta* gave Italy a respite from civil war and depredation that was far too genuine not to have called forth a literary response. But the Augustan Age, rich though it was—it gave us Livy, Horace and the best of Virgil—lasted no longer than the lifetime of Augustus himself. Anf the century that followed it is, taking it all round, admittedly second-rate. For this there are several reasons, of which one at least was the current system of education. This system, which was developed under Greek influence during the late Republic and early Empire, and retained its hold virtually unchanged until the fall of the west, concentrated—after the primary stages under the elementary teacher—on the study of classical texts, the elucidation of their form and content, and the cultivation of the art of public speaking and debate. Along with a limited number of further subjects, and crowned with the study of philosophy, this curriculum constituted the liberal arts (*artes liberales*). It was not without its merits, and it led ultimately to the mediaeval system of the *trivium* (grammar, rhetoric and dialectic) and the *quadrivium* (arithmetic, geometry, music and astronomy); but it induced an unhealthy concentration on models and traditional forms, and a progressive superficiality of thought. Typical is the craze for the archaic and the quaint, which caused the age of Hadrian to prefer Ennius to Virgil, Cato to Cicero, and saw its Greek counterpart in a movement which went back to the style of the fifth century B.C.

Yet the educational system cannot be made to bear the whole of the guilt. If rhetoric had become artificial and lacking in savour, it was partly because the real field for oratory—a free political life and free law courts—had disappeared with the establishment of the Principate. Consequently, the Silver Age of Latin Literature (A.D. 14–128) has a thwarted note; its strongest voices are the voices of protest. It had its conformists, the historian Velleius Paterculus or even a more considerable figure like the younger Pliny, whose *Letters* give a somewhat rosy picture of life about the turn of the century. But its greatest genius is revealed in the satirical prose of Tacitus, who found imperial history a congenial field in which to exercise his gift of mordant epigram, or in the bludgeoning and abuse of Juvenal's *Satires*. Already the creative powers of a Virgil are out of reach; Lucan, his nearest successor, gets his effects by rhetorical overstatement, and with a subject taken from recent history—the civil war between Caesar and Pompey (49 B.C.)—strikes home far less often than Virgil with his incomparable epic of the legendary Aeneas.

It is significant that one of the main literary occupations of the century was the compiling and recording of facts already available. This meant facts available in books; for the expansion of the late republic and early Empire went almost unreflected in the literature of the period. Later geographers still quoted Poseidonius (c. 135–51 B.C.); and Tacitus's account of the peoples of Germany is virtually unique in Latin. Of knowledge taken from books, however, the Romans of the Empire were inordinately proud. In the introduction to his *Natural History*—a vast encyclopaedia in thirty-seven books, dedicated to the Emperor Titus (A.D. 79–81)—the elder Pliny boasted that he had incorporated in his work 20,000 separate facts drawn from 100 select authors. But his critical standards fall immeasurably below those of Aristotle; and the arrangement of his work is cumbersome and unscientific. It is as if an age which had lost the power of original discovery was bent on salvaging the past, to compensate for its own lack of creativity.

Another feature of the age, which echoes the economic development, is the provenance of its writers. The centrifugal tendency which led to the decay of Italy shows itself here in the fact that increasingly it is the provinces which provide the outstanding figures. Spain especially is remarkable as the home of the two Senecas, the rhetorician and the philosopher, Lucan and perhaps Valerius Flaccus, the two chief epic poets, Columella the agronomist, Pomponius Mela the geographer, Quintilian, orator and writer on education, and the epigrammatist Martial. But just as Rome acted economically as a parasitic growth, absorbing the best from every part of the Empire, so too in the realm of literature, her magnetic influence drew anyone of ambition or ability to the centre, depriving the provinces of any chance to create their own autonomous culture. Indeed, it was only as the process of decentralization advanced that this pull exercised by Rome grew less, and the provinces—especially N. Africa and the Greek-speaking areas in the second century—began to develop again their own cultural life.

Particularly relevant to the present topic is the fact that the most advanced minds at Rome were, in the first century A.D., themselves preoccupied with the problem of decay. The Elder Pliny attributed the decline in scientific achievement to the growth of materialism, once the Empire had become united and civilized; and within the limits of the field which attracted the most widespread interest a question specifically agitating writers was the decline in oratory, a typically Roman art. It receives attention both in the *Satyricon*, a picaresque novel by Petronius, the Beau Brummel of Nero's court, and in Tacitus's *Dialogue on Orators*. Tacitus concludes that this decline springs from the setting-up of the Principate; and in his later works he develops this idea of a peace that had been bought at a heavy price, which included not only oratory, but freedom itself; even an elective monarchy, he urges, in a speech put into the mouth of the aged Emperor Galba, at the opening of a year of unparalleled civil strife and horror (A.D. 69), is only a substitute for freedom, *loco libertatis*.[1]

The first generations of the Empire lived in the consciousness of having bartered away their liberty. True, it was never liberty for more than a few: but for those few it was real enough. The Empire, however, had been inevitable, and the movement against it, led in an unorganized and spasmodic manner by individual Stoics, never got beyond the stage of obstruction and occasional conspiracy. The restoration of the republic was never seriously in question, because no one could face a return to the chaotic conditions of the first century B.C. This ambiguity of feeling in the most awakened minds, which reflected a genuine dilemma, often expressed itself in the bitterness of satire, like that of Juvenal, who 'much as he hated an arbitrary absolutism, hated equally the pettyness of mind which it bred among the people'. Like Heine, of whom these words were originally written, Juvenal made both alike the objects of his satirical shafts.

After Juvenal and Tacitus, Latin literature has little to show. The Antonine Indian Summer brought out one hothouse plant in Apuleius, the author of the fanciful novel of *The Golden Ass*; and the fourth-century Gallic renaissance could produce an Ausonius, a Christian by conversion but still writing within the pagan classical tradition, Syrian Antioch an Ammianus Marcellinus, the last of the great Roman historians, and Alexandria a poet-laureate to the emperor Honorius (A.D. 395–423), Claudian, whose

1. Tacitus, *Histories*, i, 16.

verses are at least worthy to be set beside the products of the Silver Age. Nor can one wholly ignore the compilers of manuals, Vegetius on military science, Palladius on agronomy. But for a vigorous expression of the thought of these later centuries one must turn to writers who are already representative of a new epoch with a new approach, the Christian authors and poets and the theological polemics of the Fathers of the Church. With the break-down of the State, however, Christian literature itself failed. Boethius can still write under Theoderic the Goth: but the sands were running out, and from the time of Gregory the Great at the end of the sixth century there is virtually silence for three hundred years. Yet one legacy in this realm left by the late Empire to posterity deserves mention—the invention of the *codex*, the modern book, in contrast to the ancient scroll. Favoured by the Christians, who recognized its superior advantages in facilitating the rapid consultation and adducing of texts, and by a bureaucracy which appreciated its virtues for more mundane purposes, it made a victorious progress throughout the fourth century, a forerunner of the future.

Finally the decentralization of the later Empire expresses itself in language. As the unification of the ancient world was marked by the spread of Latin and the Greek *koine* over its two halves, with a wide degree of bilingualism everywhere among educated people, and indeed among all whose business took them about the Empire, so the break-up of the Roman world was accompanied by a reversion to a monoglot east and west. Until the middle of the sixth century a knowledge of Greek lingered on among a few scholars in south Gaul; but after Boethius' attempt at a translation of Greek works into Latin, most people in the west lost the desire even to know what the Greeks had written; and Greek was left as the official language of the Byzantine court, which became increasingly cut off from the west, and the independent heir of the Hellenistic monarchies. Meanwhile Latin itself was being trans-formed. The Christians in particular, like Cicero before them, did not hesitate to reshape the language in order to render it a more suitable vehicle for their thought. St. Augustine asserted the right of the Christian to sacrifice Latinity if he thereby made his meaning clearer; and in those provinces which the barbarians overran, and where the flight from the towns and the adoption of feudalism were more wholehearted, the new movement expressed itself in the transformation of vulgar Latin into a series of new vernaculars —Italian, French, Provençal and the Spanish group.

If the history of science, religion and literature display a mingling of trends, some leading downward to decay and inanition, some forward to new ways of thinking and new forms of communication, this is even more true in other fields such as art. In portraiture the whole concept of the artist is changed. Here a prevalent mysticism found expression in an art which

looked upward, eyes fixed on heaven, and was wholly transformed for the task of presenting all temporal things from the standpoint of the transcendental;[1]

and in a striking analysis of the reliefs on the Triumphal Arch of Constantine at Rome (A.D. 315), which show the Emperor addressing the people and distributing money, a German scholar has demonstrated[2] how oriental influences, which can be perceived penetrating other cultural spheres, wherever the traditional forms weakened, have here led to an isolation of the imperial figure, a uniformity in the representation of his subjects, who are portrayed on a smaller scale, framing the emperor on either side, and finally a horizontal division of the whole field of the panel, which finds its parallel in an earlier relief showing the triumph of the Sassanid Sapor I over Valerian. To recognize this transformation is not to deny the deterioration of technique which went with it, and sprang from the break in the apprentice system by which the practical arts were transmitted. But it is the change of feeling rather than the technical incapacity which is the important thing. In architecture new forms emerge to meet the requirements of the Christian Church, the imperial courts, and the newly-endangered towns. The basilica turns inward, not outward like the classical temple.

Man appears minute in such immense, high, vaulted halls and beneath such domes; the scale of the Greek temple—always linked to earth—is overtopped; Greek laws of proportion have lost their meaning.[3]

1. E. Kornemann, op. cit. (on p. 96), p. 95.
2. H. Lietzmann, Sitzungsberichte der preussischen Akademie (Phil.-hist. Klasse), 1927, pp. 342–58.
3. H. Koch, Probleme der Spätantike, Stuttgart, 1930, p. 60.

Here too there is technical advance as well as a new concept of the relationship between God and Man.

These examples could be multiplied from other spheres—from that of the miniature, partly inspired by the form of the new *codex*, and from many arts in which, amid the relaxation and failure of vitality in the main stream, we meet a temporary renaissance of indigenous traditions, dormant beneath the overlay of Graeco-Roman culture. But these must suffice: they illustrate the essential point—the decay in the classical style and its complete transformation to express new ways of thinking and feeling, more typical of the nascent middle ages than of the ancient world.

NOTES FOR FURTHER READING

The literature of the Empire is treated in any good handbook, for instance J. Wight Duff, *A Literary History of Rome in the Silver Age*, London, 1927; for the period after Hadrian see the chapters in *Cambridge Ancient History*, Vol. XII by E. K. Rand, 'The Latin Literature of the West from the Antonines to Constantine' (pp. 571–610). Useful too is S. Dill, *Roman Society in the last century of the Western Empire*, ed. 2, London, 1899. On the religious background see G. Murray, *Five Stages of Greek Religion*, London, Thinker's Library, 1935, especially chapters IV and V; W. R. Halliday, *The Pagan Background of Early Christianity*, Liverpool, 1925; F. Cumont, *Astrology and Religion among the Greeks and Romans*, New York, 1912; and chapters in *Cambridge Ancient History*, Vol. XII, by A. D. Nock, 'The development of paganism in the Roman Empire' (pp. 409–49); by F. C. Burkitt, 'Pagan philosophy and the Christian Church' (pp. 450–75), and 'The Christian Church in the East' (pp. 476–514); and by H. Lietzmann, 'The Christian Church in the West' (pp. 515–43). On the breakdown of rationalism see E. R. Dodds, *The Greeks and the Irrational*, Berkeley and Los Angeles, 1951, especially pp. 236–55. On the development of science see the works quoted under Chapter III. On later art see G. Rodenwaldt's chapter in *Cambridge Ancient History*, Vol. XII, pp. 544–70 (with bibliography) 'The transition to Late-Classical Art'.

8

THE CAUSES OF DECLINE

To Gibbon the decline of Rome was something so natural as to require no explanation.

> The story of its ruin is simple and obvious: and instead of enquiring why the Roman Empire was destroyed we should rather be surprised that it had subsisted for so long. . . . The stupendous fabric yielded to the pressure of its own weight.[1]

Today that answer would no longer appear adequate. The stupendous fabric sinking beneath its own weight is after all a metaphor. The Roman Empire was not a building, but a state; and a phrase such as 'the pressure of its own weight' acquires meaning only when translated into a detailed analysis of various social and economic trends and forces within the Empire.

But in one respect Gibbon's formulation was one of fundamental importance; quite simply and unequivocally it broke with all cyclical, mystical-biological and metaphysical theories of decline, and stated clearly the 'naturalistic' view. The cause of decay was to be sought inside the system itself; it was not something transcendental or apocalyptic, the fulfilment of a prophecy, or a link in a sequence, fated to recur throughout eternity; nor was it something fortuitous, like the barbarian attacks (though, as we saw, these were by no means entirely fortuitous), or an error of judgement on the part of one or other of the Emperors or their respective assassins. To Gibbon the cause is something inherent, natural, and proportionate to the effect produced. This view has been amply confirmed by our own analysis. For this has shown that the Roman Empire declined not because of any one feature—the climate, the soil, the health of the population—nor indeed because of any one of those social and political factors which played so important a part in the actual process of decay, but because at a certain point it was subjected to stresses which the whole structure of ancient society had rendered it unable to withstand. In fact this society

1. E. Gibbon, *Decline and Fall of the Roman Empire*, Vol. IV, ed. J. B. Bury, 1897, p. 161; appendix following ch. 38.

was divided by contradictions which are first apparent, not in
A.D. 200, nor yet when Augustus Caesar first set up the Principate
in 27 B.C., but as early as the fifth and fourth centuries B.C., when
Athens revealed her inability to keep and broaden the middle-
class democracy she had created. The failure of Athens epitomised
the failure of the City-State. Built on a foundation of slave labour,
or on the exploitation of non-privileged groups—sometimes a
peasantry, depressed or even reduced to serfdom, sometimes the
subjects of a short-lived empire—the City-State yielded a brilliant
minority civilization. But from the start it was top-heavy. Through
no fault of its citizens, but as a result of the time and place when it
arose, it was supported by an inadequate level of technique. To
say this is to repeat a truism. The paradoxical contrast between the
spiritual achievements of Athens and her scanty material goods
has long been held up to the admiration of generations who have
found that a rich material inheritance does not automatically
ensure a corresponding richness of cultural life. But it was precisely
this low level of technique, relative to the tasks Greek and Roman
society set itself, that made it impossible even to consider dispensing
with slavery and led to its extension from the harmless sphere of
domestic labour to the mines and workshops, where it grew stron-
ger as the tensions in society grew more acute.

It is not always easy to distinguish cause from effect, when
confronted with a closely-knit texture of interacting factors. But
briefly it may be said that the Greeks of the City-State, burdened by
poverty and subjected to the constant frictions of a frontier large
in proportion to the city's area, were by tradition and necessity
aggressive and predatory; their strong feeling for autonomy tended,
on every opportunity, to slide over insensibly into a claim to
dominate others. This led to wars, which in turn took their place
among the many sources of fresh slaves. Slavery grew, and as it
invaded the various branches of production it led inevitably to the
damping down of scientific interest, to the cleavage, already
mentioned, between the classes that used their hands and the superior class that used—and was later to cease using—its mind. This
ideological cleavage thus reflects a genuine separation of the
community into classes; and henceforward it becomes the supreme
task of even the wisest sons of the City-State—a Plato and an
Aristotle—to maintain this class society, at whatever cost.

That cost was heavy. It says much for the singlemindedness

of Plato that he was willing to meet it. In the *Laws*, his last attempt to plan the just city, he produces a blue-print for implanting beliefs and attitudes convenient to authority through the medium of suggestion, by a strict and ruthless censorship, the substitution of myths and emotional ceremonies for factual knowledge, the isolation of the citizen from the outside world, the creation of types with standardized reactions, and, as a final guarantee, by the sanctions of the police-state, to be invoked against all who cannot or will not conform. It is not without reason that a French scholar, writing in 1947, characterized the later Roman Empire with 'its allegorising metaphysics, its clerical morality, its liturgical art, its threats of an inquisition, and its instruction by means of catechism, all heralding the approach of the glorious centuries of the middle ages' as 'the triumph of Plato'.[1]

For this, and no less, was the intellectual and spiritual fruit of this tree, whose roots had split upon the hard rock of technical inadequacy. Materially, increasing slavery made it all but certain that new productive forces would not be released on a scale sufficient for a radical transformation of society. Extremes of wealth and poverty became more marked, the internal market flagged, and ancient society suffered a decline in production, trade and population and, finally, the wastage of class warfare. Into this sequence the rise of the Roman Empire brought the new factor of a parasitical capital; and it spread the Hellenistic system to Italy, where agrarian pauperism went side by side with imperial expansion and domination on an unparalleled scale. In the oligarchic Rome of the senatorial regime, with its intrigues of noble houses for political power, as the gateway to prestige and wealth, a healthy development of productive forces and the deepening of cultural life was an even more remote possibility than it had been amid the turmoil of the city-state democracy or in the capitals of the Hellenistic kingdoms.

From the attempt to control and govern a political unit the size of Augustus's empire on the basis of this relatively backward material equipment arose the typical developments of the social life of the Empire—industrial dispersion, recourse to a partly natural economy within the fiscal system, continuous pressure from the court and army, and a shift of influence from the towns to the countryside—and the final attempt to retrieve the crisis, or

1. A. Piganiol, *L'Empire chrétien*, p. 401.

at least to salvage whatever could be salvaged from the ruins, by the growing use of compulsion and the machinery of the bureaucratic State. These tendencies we have already analysed, and need not repeat them here. Nor should we fall into the error of imagining that each one was inevitable in its particular place and at its particular time. Human skill and weakness played their part in postponing or accelerating the process of decay. The important point however is that the factors we have described fall together into a sequence with its own logic, and that they follow—not of course in the specific details, which were determined by a thousand personal or fortuitous factors, but in their general outlines—from the premises upon which classical civilization arose, namely an absolutely low technique and, to compensate for this, the institution of slavery. It is in these phenomena and, what is equally important, in the mental climate which they induced that we must seek the primary causes of the decline and fall of the Roman Empire.

To this view, which may seem to smack of determinism, as if it were robbing man of the right to make his own history—though in fact it merely defines the conditions within which he is free to act—the objection may be raised: *Why* was there no alternative? *Why* was the process outlined above inevitable? Why could the western Empire not have survived as did Byzantium? To take the last point first, there was, as we have said, no reason compelling the western Empire to founder *there and then*. But if we consider the Empire as it existed at the time of Augustus, and the gradual shift in emphasis from the west to the east, culminating in the final split after the reign of Theodosius (A.D. 379–95), it becomes clear that the survival of the eastern Empire really represents the saving of one part at the expense of the other; indeed the very strength of Constantinople diverted barbarian attacks to the west. It was a rump of the original which survived within the eastern provinces, as a result of the factors already discussed above (p. 93): and though its survival is itself a tribute to the efforts of the third century emperors and to the reorganization of Diocletian and Constantine, a rump it remained. When, after the lapse of several centuries, the next great step forward in European history was taken, it came, as we saw, from the west and not Constantinople.

Thus the survival of Byzantium—a part of the Empire—cannot be adduced as a sound reason for thinking that the whole might have been saved.

In fact, as more than one scholar has seen, the only way in which the west might have been preserved and enabled to advance to new achievements was by a radical change in the technical level, including communications, and a consequent transformation of the social structure. How could such a change have been effected? A little reflection will suggest two possibilities and two only. First, the upper classes might have been persuaded to abandon their privileged position, pay higher wages to the artisans, reduce the burden on the peasantry, develop technique and abolish slavery. Alternatively, the depressed classes might have seized power by a violent revolution and carried through the technical changes themselves. What chances did these two methods offer?

As regards the first, there are several valid objections to the paying of higher wages as a solution to a crisis of underconsumption under a system of free enterprise and low productivity, such as characterized the early Empire. But this is a point on which we need not linger here, since the whole history of the ruling class of the Graeco-Roman world rules out the possibility that it could for one moment have contemplated its own abdication. The thesis has only to be stated for its absurdity to become apparent. Slavery, as Aristotle, Plato, and every merchant and landowner in the ancient world knew, was natural and vital to civilization. This view not even the Christians cared to question. Like the Stoics before them they regarded all men as equally free, or equally slaves; and the issue was not one on which they ventured to challenge authority. The early Christian *Didache*, recovered only towards the end of the last century, recommends slaves to submit to their masters as to the images of God; and slaves were not to be admitted to holy orders. Thus, although individual Christians denied the right of man to enslave his fellows, in this they went beyond the teaching of the Church. It is true that manumission continued to ease the fortunes of the slave, despite legal restrictions dating back to Augustus. But by the fourth century the problem had begun to change its character with the gradual depression of other sections of society to the level of the slave. In any case by then the fatal harm was done. For centuries men's minds had been shaped by the conviction that slavery could in no circumstances be relinquished.

At this first step they stuck. For the existence of slavery made all other things—improved communications and higher forms of technique—seem superfluous.

What then of the other alternative? In one sense it was a practical issue, and a serious one, throughout Hellenistic times and the last two centuries of the Roman Republic. Social revolution was a powerful dynamic in third-century Sparta, and we know of slave risings in Pergamum, Attica, Macedon, Delos, Sicily and Italy itself, where the forces of Spartacus held the Roman legions at bay for two years (73–71 B.C.). All over the Mediterranean world the misery of the city masses united with the sufferings of the peasants to bring about spasmodic risings, which were put down with the brutality which springs from fear. From one such movement, on which was ingrafted the passion of an intensely patriotic racial minority, was born the last struggle of the Jewish people; conceived within the matrix of this struggle, with its stresses and fanatical belief in the coming kingdom, there was born the new religion of the poor and oppressed—Christianity. Two centuries later, wide-spread popular distress gave rise to similar movements of revolt. As we saw, for over a hundred years dating from the third century the Bagaudae maintained themselves in Armorica and Spain; and in north Africa, during the fourth and fifth centuries, the landless Circumcelliones, under their chieftains, the 'leaders of the saints', formed a similar movement with a religious basis—the Donatist schism—encouraging slaves to desert and terrifying the wealthier sections of the people.

On their side, the ruling classes, Greek or Roman, took every possible step to protect themselves and society. Plato had spoken[1] of cities divided as if between two armies watching each other; and his contemporary, Aeneas, who wrote on military tactics (4th century B.C.), urged the setting up of security bands from among the reliable citizens, who had most to lose from social revolution, as a defence against the mercenaries who might (as they did a century later at Carthage) run amok among their employers.[2]

But the depressed sections of society never succeeded in making any real headway, except when some member of the ruling class —an imperialist king like Cleomenes III of Sparta (c. 235–222 B.C.) or the Roman demagogues of the late Republic—exploited them for his own ends. In fact, the material basis of ancient culture was

1. Plato, *Republic*, viii, 6. 551 d.   2. Aeneas Tacticus, i, 6; xii; xiii.

inadequate for the consolidation of such a revolution, even if it could have succeeded; success must have meant chaos, and the end of the classical heritage. Indeed, even granting for argument's sake that the oppressed classes could anywhere have seized power and held it, there is no reason to think that they would have aimed at a more equalitarian form of society; the whole of classical history renders it infinitely more likely that they would merely have attempted to reverse places with their late oppressors. In any case, success was never a possibility. The lower classes were nowhere sufficiently united to make the sustained effort necessary for so gigantic a task as the expropriation of their rulers. The very existence of slavery thrust a wedge between the free artisan and the slave; and there was another cleft between the relatively prosperous domestic slave and the gangs who lived their miserable, short and brutish lives in the mines, and on the plantations and ranches. Hence the possibility of a radical change in the structure of ancient society by either of the methods we have envisaged appears extremely remote. Heitland, indeed, seems nearer the truth, when he attributes[1] the downfall of Rome to the 'Roman Fate'—using the phrase not in any metaphysical sense, but to sum up a chain of social and economic factors, which followed one upon another down to the final disintegration.

In the *General Observations on the Fall of the Roman Empire in the West* which he appended to the thirty-eighth chapter of his *Decline and Fall*, Gibbon permitted himself the following reflections on the Europe of his own day:

The balance of power will continue to fluctuate, and the prosperity of our own or the neighbouring kingdoms may be alternately exalted or depressed; but these partial events cannot essentially injure our general state or happiness, the system of arts, laws, and manners which so advantageously distinguish above the rest of mankind the Europeans and their colonies. The savage nations of the globe are the common enemies of civilised society; and we may enquire with anxious curiosity, whether Europe is still threatened with a repetition of those calamities, which formerly oppressed the arms and institutions of Rome. Perhaps the same reflections will illustrate the fall of that mighty empire, and explain the probable causes of our actual security.

It will be seen that Gibbon too is here posing a topical question: 'Is it possible that the fall of Rome may overtake our own civilization?'; and the answer which he gives, and which he supports

1. See W. E. Heitland's three pamphlets: *The Roman Fate; Iterum;* and *Last Words on the Roman Municipalities* (Cambridge: 1922, 1925 and 1928 respectively).

with arguments, is a decisive 'No!' Since his time Europe has seen two major revolutions, and a complete change in the material basis of society. It has watched war grow from the minor pastime which it was in the eighteenth century, when Sterne's Yorick could reach Paris before being reminded that he had better acquire a passport, because England and France happened to be at war, to its present-day dimensions, when it involves whole nations and counts its victims by the million. Few today would answer Gibbon's question with the same firm 'No' which satisfied the optimism of the eighteenth century. Indeed the question has a far more complicated aspect to us than it had two hundred years ago. It suggests a full investigation into the general problem of the rise and fall of civilizations—an investigation which is clearly outside the scope of the present essay.

There is, however, another topical question of more limited content, yet perhaps of more pressing urgency, which lays claim to our attention, namely 'Is it *inevitable* for western civilization to suffer the fate of Rome?' This question is urgent, because the answer we give to it will determine the character of our own actions. There is, as we have seen, a clear analogy between the methods adopted by the authoritarian state of the late Empire, and those used by similar regimes in the modern world. In both we see the demands of the State set higher than the happiness and freedom of the individual. In both a fortunate minority, well placed in the mechanism of government, can enjoy luxuries beyond the scope of the rest, for whom scarcity and hardship are a natural portion. Both foster irrational modes of thought, with new myths, dogmas, and superstitions as a substitute for reason. Moreover, it is a significant and sobering reflection that most of the advanced countries of the world, and not merely those which we call authoritarian, are experiencing a movement away from an age of *laissez faire* to one of control and state planning. From this point of view —whatever their other differences—there is a common element in the regimes of nazi Germany, communist Russia, 'capitalist' U.S.A. and the 'welfare states' of Great Britain and several other European countries. Are we then (it is sometimes asked) witnessing a new and ominous stage in our civilization, in which we must all gradually sink into a state of regimentation similar to that which heralded the end of western Rome and the birth of Byzantinism in the East? The analogies are striking and alarming, especially when we bear in mind that in its own time and context the authoritarian regime of the later Empire represented the only means of preserving the classical heritage, and was indeed the 'last hope of all friends of civilization'. Consequently, if the story of the past is to mean anything at all to the present, we are compelled to ask whether any such similar savage necessity confronts us today.

It may be said quite decisively and at once that there is no such necessity whatsoever driving the world of the twentieth century towards authoritarian tyranny. The analogies between the methods of the later empire and some of those observed in our own time may be superficially compelling; but fundamentally the modern situation is completely different. The classical world was genuinely sick of a deep-seated malady, which called forth the harsh and drastic remedies of the Caesars. But the oppressive system which sprang up piecemeal in the third and fourth centuries to meet the crises of those times was in the main a series of improvisations which can scarcely be dignified by the name of planning. Viewed as an approach towards a planned economy, even Diocletian's system, his *Edict on Prices*, his new basis for taxation and his reorganization of the provincial administration, is in practice partial, inconsistent and unco-ordinated, and very far from what is understood by an economic plan today. Indeed, an efficient planned economy could hardly have operated within the existing conditions. As a recent study has shown,[1] under the later empire not reason but personal influence and graft was what counted in the making of official decisions. It is true that the halls of power, like the higher army commands, were never closed to talent, and this fact no doubt helped to delay the collapse of the empire. But the ubiquitous system of patronage operated by governors and high civil servants in receipt of meagre salaries resulted in a network of organized corruption reminiscent of some near eastern regimes in the modern world; the great man was said to 'sell smoke', *fumum vendere*, when for a consideration he used his influence to secure a favour or an appointment. The better emperors fought hard but unsuccessfully to eradicate this abuse, which poisoned and impeded all branches of government, especially the courts. It led

1. A. H. M. Jones, *The Later Roman Empire*, I, 391–410.

to low morale and a lack of integrity in personnel which the emperors, lacking confidence in their underlings, attempted to counter
by a high degree of bureaucratic specialization, which was hardly
consistent with the primitive system of communications and so
proved on the whole to be inefficient and stultifying. Paradoxically,
this age of government interference, supervision and oppression
therefore became one in which, in the west at least, the provinces
tended more than ever before to fall apart and go their own way.

Twentieth century planning, on the other hand, represents the
complete antithesis of all this. It has followed on a general movement of emancipation, which has brought the peoples of the more
advanced countries to a greater degree of freedom and a higher
standard of living than at any time before; it is based on a much
greater understanding of economic laws and it has been made
possible only by tremendous technical improvements, including
the quickening of communications and the amelioration of methods
of instruction and information. The forces which have produced
a mental climate favourable to its adoption have been many,
varying from humanitarian theory on the one hand to the demands
of 'total' warfare and fear of the explosive character of social
distress on the other. But one thing common to all such modern
planning is a rising output and a constant increase in the technical
level of production.

In fact, the industrialization of the world in the nineteenth
and twentieth centuries has for the first time in the history of
mankind made it feasible, within the near future, from the purely
technical point of view, to feed, clothe and house the whole
of the world's population in reasonable comfort. The resources of
the machine age are capable of almost infinite expansion, and under
favourable conditions the level of production is constantly rising.
It is of course easy to point to the secular and appalling poverty
of the East. Here there are problems enough to solve, if time can
be gained to solve them. But fundamentally they are problems,
not of technique, but of social and political organization. For perhaps the most important—and obvious—contrast with ancient
Rome lies in the modern extension of technical skill and control
over nature to a point at which it has become something entirely
new and unparalleled in previous history. Thanks to machinery and
its application to the problem of communications, it has already
been possible to reduce very considerably the gap which always

existed in ancient times between town and country. Buses, bicycles, cars and trains bring the villager to town; the postal catalogue, the van, television and the cinema bring the town and city to the village. Each small town, as a Frenchman once proudly informed the writer, is now 'un petit Paris pour soi!' Electricity, the petrol engine, chemical fertilizers, and tractors, used individually or in conjunction with producers' co-operatives, are gradually, over large parts of the earth, eliminating the 'primal stupidity' of the countryside.

From the immediate point of view, however, it might appear that we are threatened by one at least of the factors which we have traced in the development of the later Empire. The tendency towards decentralization, the outward thrust of industry and commerce from the old centres, has clearly played a fundamental role in the history of western expansion. And now, as in the Roman Empire, industry exports not merely its products, but itself as well. Already in chapter three we have considered this phenomenon as one common to ancient and modern times. Because of the difference in the technical level of production in the two periods, we may not draw too close a parallel; and of course there are many new factors in the contemporary situation. For instance, our highly developed modern communications operate to prevent decentralization leading to stagnation. Instead of the primary drive outwards being followed by a secondary decentralization, breaking up the whole economic area into tiny, quasi-independent units, the scale of modern international trade and communications is such that, in spite of the political drive towards autarky, the various countries of the world are becoming more and more interdependent.

All the same, at least one of the primary factors, which have lent modern trade and imperialist expansion their peculiarly dynamic force, is also common to the economy of the Roman Empire—the need to find an external market. Like their counterparts at Rome and in the Hellenistic Age, our present-day manufacturers and merchants are obliged to look abroad for markets in which to sell the goods which their employees at home have not the money to buy. This is of course not the only reason for export drives. The situation in each country is complicated by genuine problems of the balance of trade, and in the case of highly industrialized countries such as Great Britain, by the need to buy abroad with the proceeds of its exports those foodstuffs and raw materials which cannot be grown at home. But over and above these factors there is the same need for profit as was felt by the merchants of Aquileia or Alexandria, and that magnified too by the infinitely greater amount of capital laid up in the modern instruments of production. However, in contrast to the artisans of the ancient world, the working classes of our modern industrial nations do not lack the means to buy the products of their labour for any essential and inevitable reason; for the modern world, as we saw, has almost unlimited possibilities of creating material wealth. Therefore there is no imperative reason why production should be dependent on the continual expansion of the external market, nor why, if thanks to the exporting of industry itself that external market eventually reaches saturation point, society must then necessarily decay. For the modern working class constitutes in itself a vast potential internal market; and experience has shown that with modern social planning this market can be increasingly satisfied and an economically healthy community built up on the basis of an extension of political democracy—all of which is the very opposite of the degrading and repressive system which the later Roman emperors were driven to adopt.

And what, the critic may ask, of the barbarian peril? In the happier days of the eighteenth century, when the barbarians of Asia were fast being introduced to civilization, Gibbon could give a confident answer to this question.

From the Gulf of Finland to the Eastern Ocean, Russia now assumes the form of a powerful and civilized empire. The plough, the loom, and the forge, are introduced on the banks of the Volga, the Oby, and the Lena; and the fiercest of the Tartar hordes have been taught to tremble and obey. The reign of independent barbarism is now contracted to a narrow span; and the remnant of the Calmucks or Uzbecks, whose forces may be almost numbered, cannot seriously excite the apprehensions of the great republic of Europe.[1]

If today we are less confident, it is because we are less sure about what constitutes barbarism. Modern war now depends so entirely on science and industry, that no barbarian people could threaten civilization without first acquiring a high degree of material civilization itself. But can we be sure that the possession of the plough, the loom and the forge—to say nothing of the jet fighter

1. Gibbon, *op. cit.* Vol. IV, ed. Bury, p. 164.

and the hydrogen bomb—are sufficient guarantee that their owners will also automatically exhibit a high degree of civilized behaviour? Is there not in fact a danger of making a superficial equation between technical efficiency and civilization? If we use the term barbarian in the sociologist's sense to describe the cultural level below that of civilized man, then the danger from barbarians is clearly past. Even feudal Japan was able to offer a serious threat to the western powers only because it modified its traditional structure by adopting the productive techniques of a modern industrial society. But not only feudal Japan, but nations in the very heart of civilized Europe have recently shown how dangerously easy it is to slip back from everything which is most to be valued in our cultural heritage. A salutary and painful lesson has been taught us that barbarism in this sense remains a danger at all times, and in all societies, and that the price of civilization, like that of freedom, is eternal vigilance.

However, these considerations seem to establish the point that there is nothing inevitable about authoritarian tyranny. While it would be trespassing on the field of prophecy to state with assurance that the modern world *will* escape the fate of Rome, we may assert without hesitation that it lies in our power to avoid such a fate, and indeed that it is our duty, knowing this, to exert ourselves against any tendencies in our own society which resemble those predominating in the late Empire and which, if unchecked, could lead us too to simulate a disease that might eventually become real—and fatal. The essential difference between the modern welfare state and the later Roman Empire can only lie in the real content of the word 'welfare'. It is this real content to which we must look as our criterion, for the cynic can easily point out that the vocabulary of 'welfare' was among the commonest used in the official proclamations of the later emperors, who professed only to be anxious to augment their subjects' prosperity by exercising generosity and humanity; and on the other hand there have been recent examples of modern states making similar professions while in practice merely guaranteeing advantages for the few at the expense of the many.

Here we have broached only one out of the many problems

which confront us today—problems of international war, of communities at various levels of economic, social and moral development, of the awakening of subject peoples, of nationalism, and of imperialism, and even of our possibly destroying the planet on which we live—problems which fall outside the scope of this essay. However, the result of our comparison suggests a qualified and cautious optimism concerning the solution of this one issue at least. For we have seen that authoritarian repression and the caste state are not the inevitable fate in store for us, as they were for the Caesars, the rulers of a world that was materially backward, and split from top to bottom by the curse of slave labour. The future offers something brighter than that.

NOTES FOR FURTHER READING

The books mentioned after Chapter I are all relevant to the subject matter of this chapter. The financing and organizing of the Byzantine State, and its contrast with western Europe, are treated in a stimulating fashion by L. M. Hartmann in an essay translated by H. Liebeschütz under the title *The Early Mediaeval state: Byzantium, Italy and the West*, London (Historical Association), 1949. The problem of reconstructing the society of the Roman Empire is raised by F. Oertel in *Cambridge Ancient History*, Vol. XII, pp. 253 ff.

9

THE REALITY OF PROGRESS

THE Western Empire perished; but it did not leave Europe where the Achaean invaders found her. Similarly, there is a vast difference between the Europe of the twentieth century, for all its experience of regimentation and oppression, and the Rome or Byzantium of Constantine. The harsh regime of the later Emperors achieved its object, in preserving the classical heritage for posterity. Man is not bound to a revolving wheel. Progress is real.

The Abbé Galliani, in a letter of January 1st, 1744, asked

The fall of empires? What can that mean? Empires being neither up nor down do not fall. They change their appearance, and it is people who speak of overthrow and ruin—words which hide the whole game of error and deception. It would be more correct to speak of *phases* of empire.

In this paradoxical view—the denial of the whole process of decline and fall—there is a modicum of truth. It has been defended with great vigour by Dopsch and Heichelheim, who point out with justice that there was no complete break in any of the main branches of human activity. The process to which we give the name 'decline and fall' lasted over several centuries, and it brought decay in the intensity of economic life and culture generally. Over large areas, as we saw, the influence of the towns weakened and lapsed, and life continued on the land. Nevertheless the main tradition persisted. It can even be argued that the cultural decline which preceded the collapse of the western imperial authority brought the Romans nearer to the level of their conquerers, and so facilitated the eventual transfer of the legacy. The extent of this transfer varied of course from area to area. In the south, where the Germans were never more than a minority—in Italy, Provence, Aquitania and Spain—the old population remained, and the new-comers were absorbed: Romance languages, not Germanic, took the place of Latin. But in the zone represented by Britain, the Netherlands and Belgium, and the Rhine and Danube frontiers, the process was more complicated, and differed for almost every activity. For here there were mass German settlements, and the original Romans either fled south in the early fifth century, when the court abandoned Trier, or were decimated if they remained behind. We can read in Salvian of the distress of one of his kins-women, who had lost all her property and had to go out cleaning for Frankish ladies. However, even here the crafts and techniques persisted. When we speak of economic decline, we speak of organ-izational decline, not of the complete disappearance of activities and skills. Indeed, although most of the amenities and graces of life disappeared for that minority which had formerly enjoyed them, the actual techniques remained, almost unchanged, passed on from father to son inside the rigid corporations of the later Empire. In the Greek parts of the Empire the cities still continued to exist, though shrivelled in size; in the West, though the cities often (though not always) died, feudal estates and monasteries guarded the legacy and transmitted it.

There had been feudalism and temple estates in the ancient world before—in Babylon for instance. But the feudalism which bridged the gap detween the decline of the Roman Empire and the new rise of capitalistic production for the market, which ushered in the modern world, was infinitely more fruitful than its earlier counterparts. The reason for this was that it had behind it, giving it strength, the achievement of classical civilization and its tech-nical heritage. The new arts and crafts introduced by the Greeks and Romans survived. In France and Germany the furnaces of the Syrian glass-workers were kept going by their followers, who passed the technique down from craftsman to apprentice; and by A.D. 700 water-wheels, known in the first century, and developed in the fourth, were being widely used as far north as England. One should not indeed ignore the positive contributions of the invaders themselves.[1] Fur coats and trousers had become sufficient-ly popular garments to be forbidden at Rome by imperial edict in A.D. 397 and 399; and the early middle ages had the benefit of a whole series of innovations which they owed, not to the classical world, but to the northerners, including cloisonné jewellery, felt-making, the ski, the use of soap and butter, the construction of tubs and barrels, the cultivation of rye, oats, spelt and hops, and the discovery of the heavy plough, the stirrup and the horseshoe. But these inventions mainly served to supplement the main legacy,

1. Cf. L. White, *Speculum*, xv, 1940, 144 f.

and it was on the achievements of the classical world that the Middle Ages built, and went forward to a widespread use of animal, water and wind power. The significance of these new developments in the story of mankind is incalculable. It has been remarked and not without some truth, that

the chief glory of the later Middle Ages was not its cathedrals or its epics or its scholasticism: it was the building for the first time in history of a complex civilisation which rested not on the backs of sweating slaves or coolies, but primarily on non-human power.[1]

This achievement, like all else which mediaeval Europe accomplished, is inconceivable without the classical heritage on which it is founded.

To describe the transmission of this heritage is no simple matter. In the first place the lowest point was naturally not reached with the collapse of the imperial power in A.D. 476. There is a period of wastage often lasting over several centuries; and in some spheres this process is still continuing, while in others recovery has already begun. What was rooted in the soil lived on—the cultivation of the vine, the old boundaries, the town walls, the buildings. But often the cultural background, for instance the life which went on within the material town structures, was completely changed. Often more was lost than is at first sight obvious, and was later regained by cultural transference. But gradually the process of recovery gathered speed; and many separate channels and tributaries eventually combined to form that mighty stream which is our classical heritage of today.

The manors and monasteries of western Europe have already been mentioned as the centres of technical skill; but the monasteries at least were more. As homes of learning where the Latin tongue was still spoken, they housed the work of hundreds of monks, who sedulously copied out the ancient classical texts which were to serve as the foundation of the new learning with the coming of the Renaissance. The fall of the western Roman government had proved a severe blow to Roman Law in the west. During the sixth century the Germans were still concerned to make transcripts for

1. L. White, *ibid.* 156.

their Roman subjects; and in France and Germany the so-called
Breviary of Alaric, a simplified version published in A.D. 506 for
those who could not cope with the full codes, was in force until
the twelfth century. But in Spain the distinction between German
and Roman Law had broken down as early as the seventh century.
In this field the eastern Empire came to the rescue, and from the
eleventh century onwards the rediscovery of Justinian's *Corpus
Iuris Civilis* 'spread the study of Roman Law like wildfire through
the nascent universities of Europe, indeed was often a cause of
their foundation'.[1] Thus reborn, Roman Law became, in Maine's
words, the *lingua franca* of jurisprudence. It served to establish a
common basis of law over the greater part of Europe. By this time
the dark ages were past, and the fresh breezes of the twelfth
century fanned the sparks of culture and learning into a fresh flame.

Meanwhile in the eastern half of the Empire, the Byzantine
State preserved both classical theory and classical techniques.
Thence both passed to the Sassanid Empire of Iran and to the
Kalifs of Baghdad, to be temporarily incorporated in the swirling
flood of Islam. The Arabs in turn carried the heritage back through
the old Roman lands of North Africa, and passed it on to the Moorish provinces of Spain and Sicily. Thus enriched, it returned to
Europe, to be re-united with the direct stream of tradition in the
west. From the time of the Renaissance and the rediscovery of
Greek it became difficult to separate the old direct heritage from
what had been newly unearthed and absorbed. Here it is sufficient
to observe that this legacy was passed on to fertilize the minds of
those who were building a new world, based on experimental
science and improved techniques, along the Atlantic seaboard.
Thence it spread to both shores of that ocean and to the remotest
parts of the modern world. From that fertilization our present
civilization has sprung, the heir of the ancient world by a devious
but unbroken line of descent.

In one way or another our own society has incorporated within its
texture all that matters of classical culture and the culture of still
earlier civilizations. The decline and fall of Rome is real enough,
a genuine decay springing from a complex of causes that are only

1. F. de Zulueta, 'The Science of Law' in *The Legacy of Rome*, p. 177.

too painfully clear. Yet, for all that, it was the route along which humanity passed, through the long apparent stagnation of feudalism to that fresh burst of progress, which created the modern world. And now, having advanced, not indeed along the straight upward line of which we spoke in an earlier chapter, but by the time honoured method of one step backwards, two steps forwards, we find ourselves once more standing at the crossroads and turning with Gibbon to read anew the lesson of the decline of Rome.

'This awful revolution' he wrote 'may be usefully applied to the instruction of the present age.' What then are the alternatives which it indicates for us? They are reasonably clear. One choice that confronts us is to attempt to plan the resources of modern society for the whole of its peoples, whatever their colour; to press forward towards a more equitable distribution of wealth, both nationally and on an international scale; and to give full scope for the employment of the new technical forces man already controls. This is a new path along which antiquity cannot light us, because it never trod that way. The alternative is to ignore the lesson which the history of Rome offers, to follow in the footsteps of the ancient world (which never solved this problem because it could not) by planning or failing to plan—for the few, for underconsumption at home, for a scramble after markets abroad and so eventually for imperial or colonial wars, revolutions and ultimate ruin.

That this ruin might, like that of Rome, give rise to new social developments, leading in the fullness of time to some future society, which would in turn be presented with the same problem, is little consolation to us if we fail to solve it now. But because we have the choice, where the ancients had none, we may properly exercise some degree of charity as we contemplate their downfall and the inexorable chain of cause and effect, as it operated within the social structure of antiquity; and instead of solacing ourselves with the passing of moral judgements on men long since dead, we shall do better to be quite sure that we understand why ancient society declined to an inevitable end. Having learnt the lessons of that 'awful revolution', we can more advantageously devote our passions and our energies to the amelioration of what is wrong in our own society.

NOTES FOR FURTHER READING

The problem of whether there is a break or continuity between the late western Empire and mediaeval Europe, and if there is a break, when it comes, has been discussed by A. Dopsch, *Economic and Social Foundations of European Civilisation*, London, 1937; by J. Pirenne, *Economic and Social History of Mediaeval Europe*, London, 1936; by F. Lot, *The End of the Ancient World and the beginning of the Middle Ages*, New York, 1932; and by H. St. L. B. Moss, *The Birth of the Middle Ages*, Oxford, 1935. Pirenne subsequently returned to the argument in *Mohammed and Charlemagne*, London, 1939. For readers of German, H. Aubin's volume of essays *Vom Altertum zum Mittelalter*, Munich, 1949, provides a useful survey of some of the problems of the period of transition. See also the collection of essays on the transformation of the Roman world, edited by Lynn White, which is quoted on p. 9, n. 1.

TABLE OF DATES

B.C.

44   Caesar assassinated.

31   Battle of Actium; Octavian, victor over Antony and
     Cleopatra, henceforth master of the Roman World.

27   Octavian given the title of Augustus. He makes a gesture of
     'restoring the republic'. Institution of the Empire generally
     dated from this year.

GREEK AND ROMAN WRITERS
MENTIONED IN THIS BOOK

HERODOTUS (c. 484–c. 425 B.C.), Greek historian of the Persian Wars.

THUCYDIDES (fl. 430–400 B.C.), Greek historian of the great war between Athens and Sparta.

PLATO (427–347 B.C.), Greek philosopher, founder of the Academy.

ARISTOTLE (384–322 B.C.), Greek philosopher and scientist, founder of the Lyceum.

AENEAS (4th cent. B.C.), Greek writer of tactics.

EPICURUS (342–270 B.C.), Greek philosopher, founder of the Garden.

ELDER CATO (234–149 B.C.), Roman statesman, historian and writer on agriculture.

POLYBIUS (c. 200–118 B.C.), Greek historian of Rome's rise to power.

POSEIDONIUS (c. 135–51 B.C.), Greek philosopher active at Rome.

JULIUS CAESAR (100–44 B.C.), writer of commentaries describing his campaigns in Gaul and the Civil War.

CICERO (106–43 B.C.), Roman statesman, orator and philosopher.

SERVIUS SULPICIUS (d. 43 B.C.), Roman jurisconsult and friend of Cicero.

LUCRETIUS (98–55 B.C.), composed the *De Rerum Natura*, a Latin epic designed to rid men of the fear of death, based on Epicurus's teachings.

CATULLUS (87–c. 47 B.C.), Roman poet, writer of lyrics, epigrams and short epic poems.

STRABO (c. 64 B.C.–c. A.D. 24), Greek geographer.

VIRGIL (70–19 B.C.), Roman epic poet, composed the *Aeneid*.

HORACE (65–8 B.C.), Roman satirist and lyric poet.

ELDER SENECA (c. 55 B.C.–c. A.D. 40), Roman writer on rhetoric.

VELLEIUS PATERCULUS (c. 19 B.C.–c. A.D. 30), minor Roman historian.

YOUNGER SENECA (c. 4 B.C.–A.D. 65), Roman philosopher, tragedian and satirist.

ELDER PLINY (A.D. 23–79), Roman encyclopaedist.

LUCAN (A.D. 39–65), Roman epic poet, author of the *De Bello Civili*, an epic on the war between Caesar and Pompey.

PETRONIUS (d. A.D. 66), Roman satirist.

COLUMELLA (fl. A.D. 50), Roman writer on agriculture.

POMPONIUS MELA (fl. A.D. 44), Roman geographer.

QUINTILIAN (c. A.D. 35–c. 100), Roman writer of rhetoric and education.

MARTIAL (c. A.D. 40–c. 104), Roman writer of epigrams.

VALERIUS FLACCUS (*d. c.* A.D. 90), Roman epic poet, wrote a poem on the Argonauts.

YOUNGER PLINY (A.D. 61–*c.* 113), Roman letter-writer; his works include his correspondence with the Emperor Trajan whilst he was governor of Bithynia.

DIO CHRYSOSTOM (*c.* A.D. 40–after 112), Greek orator and Cynic philosopher.

TACITUS (*c.* A.D. 55–*c.* 118), Roman historian, author of the *Germania*, *Histories*, *Annals*, etc.; also a dialogue on the decay of oratory.

JUVENAL (*fl.* A.D. 100), Roman satirist.

APELEIUS (*fl.* 2nd cent. A.D.), Roman novelist, author of the *Golden Ass*.

AELIUS ARISTIDES (A.D. 117–189), Greek rhetorician and sophist.

TERTULLIAN (*c.* A.D. 160–*c.* 225), Latin church writer from Africa.

PLOTINUS (A.D. 205–270), Greek Neoplatonist philosopher.

ULPIAN (*d.* A.D. 228), Roman jurist.

AUSONIUS (*fl.* 4th cent. A.D.), Roman poet and teacher of grammar and rhetoric from Bordeaux.

AMMIANUS MARCELLINUS (*fl.* 4th cent. A.D.), Roman historian.

PALLADIUS (*fl.* 4th cent. A.D.), Latin writer on agriculture and veterinary science.

LIBANIUS (*fl.* 4th cent. A.D.), Greek orator and writer from Syria.

THEMISTIUS (*fl.* 4th cent. A.D.), Greek scholar who paraphrased Aristotle.

EUSEBIUS (*c.* A.D. 260–340), Greek Church historian from Caesarea in Palestine.

VEGETIUS (*fl.* A.D. 386), Latin writer on the art of war.

LACTANTIUS (*fl.* 4th cent. A.D.), Latin Christian writer.

ST. AUGUSTINE (A.D. 354–430), Latin Christian writer.

ST. JEROME (A.D. 346–420), Latin Christian writer, translator of the Latin Bible (the Vulgate).

OROSIUS (*fl.* A.D. 410–420), Latin church historian from Spain and pupil of St. Augustine.

CLAUDIAN (*fl. c.* A.D. 400), Latin court poet, originally from Alexandria.

SALVIAN (*fl.* 5th cent. A.D.), presbyter of Marseilles, and Latin Christian writer.

BOETHIUS (*c.* A.D. 480–534), Christian philosopher and writer in various fields.

THE ROMAN EMPERORS TO THEODOSIUS

27 B.C.–A.D. 14	Augustus		
A.D.		A.D.	
14–37	Tiberius	238–244	Gordian III
37–41	Gaius (Caligula)	244–249	Philip
41–54	Claudius	249–251	Decius
54–68	Nero	251–253	Trebonianus
68–69	Galba	253	Aemilianus
69	Otho	253–260	Valerianus
69	Vitellius	253–268	Gallienus
69–79	Vespasian	268–270	Claudius Gothicus
79–81	Titus	270–275	Aurelian
81–96	Domitian	275–276	Tacitus
96–98	Nerva	276	Florianus
98–117	Trajan	276–282	Probus
117–138	Hadrian	282–283	Carus
138–161	Antoninus Pius	283–285	Carinus
161–180	Marcus Aurelius	283–284	Numerianus
161–169	L. Verus	284–305	Diocletian
180–193	Commodus	286–305	Maximian
193	Pertinax	292–306	Constantius
193	Didius Julianus	293–311	Galerius
193–211	Septimius Severus	306–312	Maxentius
211–217	Caracalla	311–323	Licinius
211–212	Geta	306–337	Constantine
217–218	Macrinus	337–340	Constantine II
218–222	Elagabalus	337–361	Constantius II
222–235	Severus Alexander	337–350	Constans
235–238	Maximinus	361–363	Julian
238	Gordian I	363–364	Jovian
238	Gordian II	364–375	Valentinian I
238	Balbinus	364–378	Valens
238	Pupienus	367–383	Gratian
		375–392	Valentinian II
		379–395	Theodosius

Emperors whose names are bracketed held joint rule.
The following later emperors are also mentioned in the text.

395–423   Honorius
475–476   Romulus Augustulus
527–565   Justinian (Eastern
                Empire)

INDEX

This map shows the Roman Empire at the death of Trajan, when it achieved its greatest extension, except in Britain, where, for some decades of the second century, the frontier lay along the Clyde-Forth line. The provinces east of the Euphrates were abandoned by Hadrian, but at various times later the Romans held territory in the Euphrates bend.

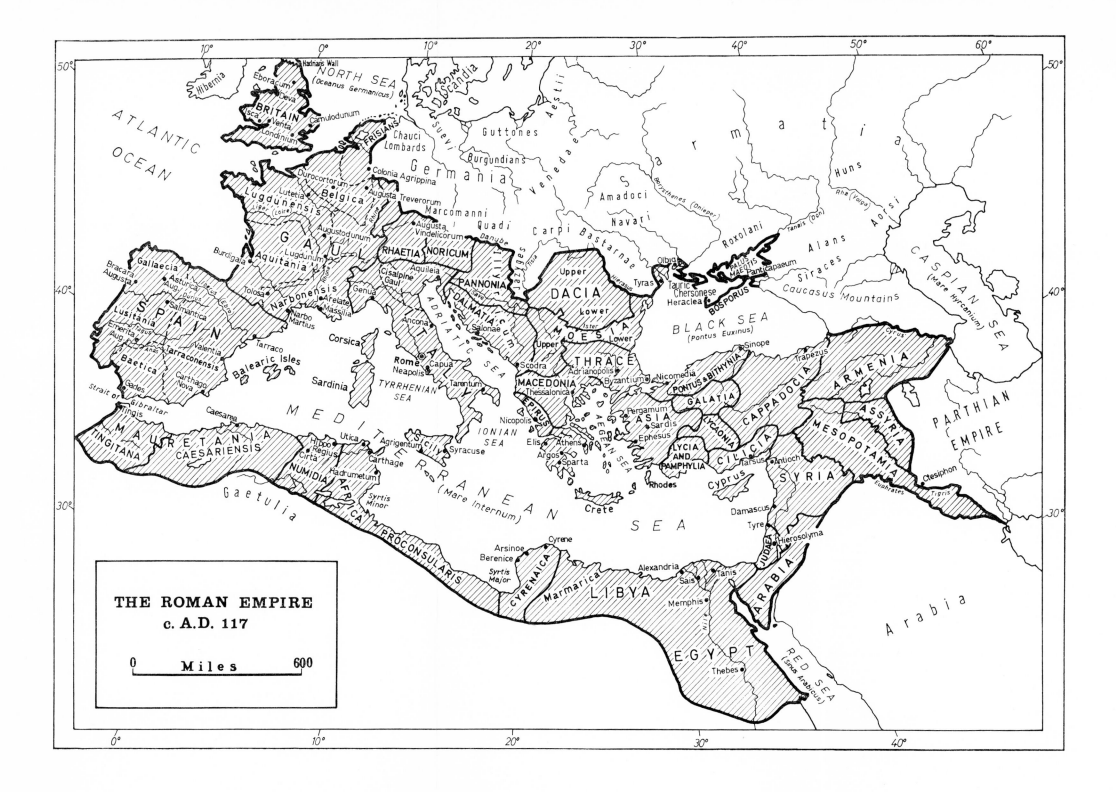

THE ROMAN EMPIRE
c. A.D. 117

0   Miles   600